Developing

COMPREHENSION SKILLS

CLARE CONSTANT · DAVID KITCHEN

Heinemann Educational Publishers
Halley Court, Jordan Hill, Oxford OX2 8EJ
A division of Reed Educational & Professional Publishing Ltd

OXFORD MELBOURNE AUCKLAND
JOHANNESBURG BLANTYRE GABORONE
IBADAN PORTSMOUTH (NH) USA CHICAGO

First published 1997

05 04 03 02
14 13 12

ISBN 0 435 10432 2

Designed and typeset by Ken Vail Graphic Design, Cambridge
Cover photograph: Tony Stone
Cover design: Miller Craig and Cocking
Photo research: Valerie Mulcahy
Printed and bound in Edinburgh by Scotprint

Acknowledgements

We should like to thank the following for permission to reproduce copyright material:

Advertisement on p6: Optimax Laser Eye Clinics; extract on p11 from *The Eighteenth Emergency* by Betsy Byars. Copyright © 1973 by Betsy Byars. Used by permission of Viking Penguin, a division of Penguin Books USA, Inc; 'Graffiti's Here, OK?', p12, slightly amended from *The Blue Peter Green Book* by Lewis Bronze, Nick Heathcote and Peter Brown: BBC Books; extract from *The World of Festivals* by Phillip Steele on p15: Macdonald Young Books; article on p19: News Team International Ltd; 'With nowhere to live...', pp20–21: Shelter, The National Campaign for Homeless People; advertisement for Effico Tonic on p23: Pharmax HealthCare Ltd; 'I'll be your best friend' advertisement on p23: The National Canine Defence League; extract from *Writing Home* by Alan Bennet on p24: Faber and Faber Ltd; advertisement for Acorn Stairlifts on p26: Brahm, Leeds; 'the experience of a lifetime!' advertisement on p26 reproduced by kind permission of the British Heart Foundation; charity notice for the Dystonia Society on p27: the Dystonia Society; 'Talking Newspapers for the Blind' charity notice on p27: Talking Newspapers Association UK; extract from *Madame Doubtfire* on pp32–33 copyright © by Anne Fine. Reproduced by permission of Penguin Books Ltd; article by Rebecca Holmes on p34: *Daily Express*; 'Steam Shovel', p35 is from *Upper Pasture* by Charles Malam, Copyright 1930, © 1958 by Charles Malam. Reprinted by permission of Henry Holt and Co, Inc; 'Old Mister Roberts' by Tony Charles, p38: HarperCollins Publishers Ltd; extract from *Rags and Riches* by Joan Lingard on pp45–46: Hamish Hamilton Ltd; extract from *The Monster Garden* by Vivien Alcock on pp48–49: Methuen Children's Books; 'Biking free' by Pie Corbett, p52: HarperCollins Publishers Ltd; extract (abridged) from *And when did you last see your father?* by Blake Morrison on p54 reprinted by permission of the Peters, Fraser and Dunlop Group Ltd; 'The 2-minute call that saved her life', pp57–60 reproduced by kind permission of Help the Aged; 'Diary of a survivor aged 8 1/2', pp62–63: Christian Aid; extract from *The Cockatrice Boys* by Joan Aiken on pp66–67: Victor Gollancz Ltd; article by Lesley Gerard on pp70–71: *The Independent*; extract from *Ganging Up* by Alan Gibbons on pp80–83: Orion Children's Books; article by Arabella Warner on pp86–87: *The Independent*; 'What the Teacher Said When Asked: What Er We Avin for Geography Miss?' by John Agard, p90 is from *Can I Buy a Slice of Sky?* published by Hodder Children's Books, 1996. Reproduced by kind permission of John Agard, c/o Caroline Sheldon Literary Agency; extract from *Granny the Pag* (Hamish Hamilton Children's Books, 1995) on pp93–95 copyright © 1995 by Nina Bawden. Reproduced by permission of Penguin Books Ltd; extract from *No Turning Back* on pp97–99 copyright © by Beverley Naidoo. Reproduced by permission of Penguin Books Ltd; 'This tube would save their sight', p103 reproduced by kind permission of Sight Savers International; extract from *Bitter Herbs* by Marga Minco, translated from the Dutch by Roy Edwards on pp105–07 © OUP, 1960. Reproduced by permission of Oxford University Press; 'Throwing a Tree', p110 is from *The Complete Poems* by Thomas Hardy, edited by James Gibson (Papermac); extract on pp113–15 © 1993 by K M Peyton. Extracted from *The Boy Who Wasn't There*, published by Corgi, a division of Transworld Publishers Ltd. All rights reserved; article on pp118–19 © York Membery / *The Times*, 1996; extract from *The Country Girls* on pp122–24 copyright © Edna O'brien; extract from *Three Moons in Vietnam* by Maria Coffey on pp126–28: Little, Brown and Co; extract from *Edith Jackson* by Rosa Guy on pp142–44 first published by Victor Gollancz Ltd; article by Nicki Pope on pp146–47: *Today* newspaper; extract from *The Guilty Party* by Joan Lingard on pp149–51: Hamish Hamilton Ltd; 'Look forward to a better future', pp153–57: Friends of the Earth.

The Publishers have made every effort to trace the copyright holders, but if they have inadvertently overlooked any, they will be pleased to make the necessary arrangements at the first opportunity.

The Publishers should like to thank the following for permission to reproduce photographs on the pages noted.

Camera Press/Benoit Gysembergh 8R; J Allan Cash 8L; Tony Stone Images: Stewart Cohen 8B, Bruce Hands 119; The Hutchison Library/Pierrette Collomb 13; News Team International Ltd 19; National Canine Defence League (NCDL) 23; Express Newspapers plc/Douglas Morrison 34; The Image Bank/Steve Satushek 52; Help the Aged/Marcella Hugard 57, 58; Christian Aid/Achinto 62; Sight Savers International, Royal Commonwealth Society for the Blind 103; News International Syndication: Ken Lennox 146T, *Today Newspapers* 146B; The Hulton Getty Collection 147.

Introduction

This book aims to help you to develop your reading and understanding skills so that you can respond confidently to the texts you meet in Key Stage 3, in your tests and later in your GCSE classes.

As you have already found out, some texts are easy to understand, but others are much more complicated. You may have wondered:

- what makes this text seem so interesting and that one so boring?
- what do you do when a text seems impossible to understand?
- where do you start when you are reading a poem?
- how can you cope if you have only got a short time to work out what a text is about and answer all the questions on it?

The purpose of this book is to help you discover the answers to these and many other questions about reading and understanding texts. You will find that it is far more than just a 'test preparation' book. Using it will ensure you can deal confidently with any type of reading matter *and* enjoy what you read.

Section A teaches the essential skills you need to read a wide range of texts.

Section B offers practice units containing fiction, non-fiction, poetry, drama, information and media texts. The texts and questions become increasingly demanding throughout this section.

Section C contains texts and questions for practice in timed conditions.

Contents

Section C: Tests

Everywhere you look – on roads, in shops, at home, in school – you are bombarded by words. But did you realise that all pieces of writing have two things in common?

1 They are aimed at an **audience**: the person or group of people that the writer hopes will read the text.

2 They are written for a **purpose**: a writer wants the audience to respond in some way to what they have read.

Look carefully at each of the following pieces of writing.

A

B

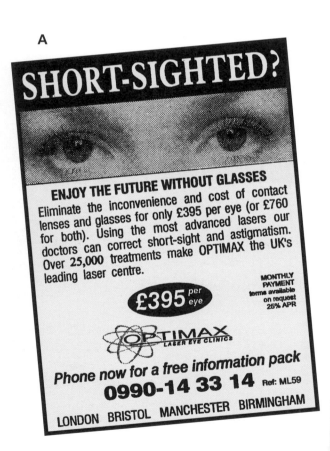

C

FIVE-MINUTE BANANA CAKE

If your kids think eating healthily means being force fed rabbit food, then change their minds by offering them a slice of this delicious low-fat banana cake.

Ingredients

5 large bananas (peeled)
5 oz raw cane sugar
2 beaten eggs
8 oz wholemeal flour
3 tsp baking powder

Mash the bananas. Stir in the sugar and eggs, before folding in the flour and baking powder. Add a little milk if it seems too stiff.

Pour the mixture into a small loaf tin and bake at 180°C for 1 hour 15 minutes.

Turn out onto a wire rack and allow to cool.

D

Ink: a coloured liquid used for drawing, printing and writing. Originally only blue in colour, later permanent black too. Made traditionally from gallic and tannic acids. Synthetic dyes are used to produce modern ink.

It was the clatter of hooves that first told him the Stark brothers had ridden into town. Grit and tumbleweed kicked up in the street like billows of autumn mist, but the townsfolk were vanishing like snow in July. Touching the brim of his stetson Dirk offered a 'Howdy Ma'am,' to Miss Millie as she rushed past him. Then, his spurs tapping as they traced a scorpion's path across the dust, he marched along the wooden verandah and into the saloon.

E

Activity

For each piece of writing discuss:

1   What is the writing about?

2   Who is it written for?
(Who is the audience?)

3   How does it try to make that audience respond?
(What is the purpose?)

Make sure you explain why you think your answers to **2** and **3** are right.

 Remember

These are good questions to ask yourself about any text you read. They will help you to gain an overview of what a text is about before you study it in more detail.

Mix and match

Suiting the audience and purpose matters so much to authors that they will produce very different pieces of work even when they are writing about the same subject.

On these pages are some photographs, some headings and two pieces of text written by the same author.

Match the right photograph, heading, and text to make each of these articles.

1 An article aimed at young people. Its purpose is to encourage them to come to a FoodAid fundraising event.

2 An article for adults. Its purpose is to encourage them to sell tickets at a FoodAid fundraising event.

Explain how you made your choices.

Pictures

a

b

c

Headings

a

It's a Stikki Business

b

Feasting to Stop Famine?

c

You Can Make A Difference

Texts

a

Ever felt frustrated and helpless after seeing horrific reports about famine victims on the news? You're not alone, but if you can spare a few hours on Saturday 25th July to sell tickets on the door for this year's Beggar's Banquet at Brookwood Leisure Centre you could make a real difference to their lives.

The annual event is expected to be attended by over 700 local young people this year as teen idol Stikki Momentz has agreed to play both host and chef while top band Red Peppers play the night away. All proceeds will go to FoodAid's Rwanda project to provide food and medicine parcels …

b

It could be you …

feasting and dancing the night away at this year's Beggar's Banquet. All you have to do is buy a raffle ticket (minimum donation £5.00). Then at 7.00 pm you could be one of ten lucky winners having their names drawn out of the begging bowl.

The prize? A banquet prepared before your very eyes by a top TV personality. Yes, you've guessed it – that dangerous comedian

Stikki Momentz

is not only hosting the show, he's doing the catering too!

Even if you lose, the famous Red Peppers will be playing as you dine on bread and water before dancing the night away …

What's the difference?

Compare the text you thought would suit an adult with the one you thought would suit a young person. Then copy out and finish the chart below to show the main differences in the way they are written to suit their audiences.

Differences	Adult's text	Young person's text
The way it is written: • words used • sentences/paragraphs	harder words like …	sentences are shorter and …
Mood	serious, because it says …	

A2 Reading prose

When you first look at a prose text, it is easy to be put off by the mass of words on the page. If you follow the four steps below, with a little practice you will soon feel confident about approaching prose.

1 Have a quick read through

Start by quickly reading through the whole text.

Do not worry too much if you cannot understand every single word or if you miss a few of the details at this stage. You are simply trying to gain a rough picture of what the text is about and the order in which it is written.

2 Know what you have to find out

If you are going to answer questions about the text, now is the time to read them through carefully.

Make sure you are clear about what it is you are looking for, before going back to re-read the text.

3 Work out where the answers will be

Now, using what you learned on your first read through, read the text again. You should find that:
- you are starting to understand it better
- you are able to spot where you will find your answers.

4 Read in detail

Finally, focus on those parts of the text where you are sure the answers can be found. Study them carefully, and read **thoroughly and thoughtfully**. Try to:
- work out exactly what is going on
- work out the meaning of any difficult words (look at pages 39–41 for ideas on how to do this)
- think about the way the text is written (as you work through Sections A and B you will learn how to do this).

Fiction

Fiction is prose which deals with 'made up' events, such as stories. As you might expect, one of the main purposes of fiction is to **entertain**.

Read the passage below, then answer the questions that follow.

In this story a boy whose nickname is Mouse is worried that some boys from his school are going to beat him up. His mother is talking to him about it.

Mouse

'Come to supper,' Mouse's mother called. He went into the kitchen where his mother was putting food on the table. She sat down, spread a paper napkin on her lap and said, 'Why doesn't Ezzie help you with those boys?'

'What?'

5   'Why doesn't Ezzie help you fight those boys?' she repeated, nodding her head towards the window.

'Oh, Mom.'

'I mean it. If there were *two* of you, then those boys would think twice before –'

10   'Oh Mom!' He bent over his plate and began to smash his lima beans with his fork. He thought about it for a moment, of stepping in front of Marv Hammerman and Tony Lionni and the boy in the black sweat shirt and saying in a cool voice, 'I think I'd better warn you that I've got my friend with me.'

'Who's your friend?'

15   '*This* is my friend.' At that Ezzie would step out of the shadows and stand with him.

Marv Hammerman would look at them, sizing them up, the two of them, this duo his mother had created for strength. Then with a faint smile Hammerman would reach out, grab them up like cymbals and clang them 20 together. When Hammerman set them down they would twang for forty-five minutes before they could stumble off.

The Eighteenth Emergency by Betsy Byars

Questions

1   What is Mouse having for his supper?

2   How does Mouse's mother suggest he should deal with his problem?

3   Why doesn't Mouse think his mother's plan will work?

4   How does the writer make Hammerman seem powerful?

5   What kind of person is Mouse shown to be in this passage?

Non-fiction

Non-fiction is prose which deals with real events, people, places and facts. Examples of non-fiction are diaries, advertisements, reports, travel writing, leaflets, biographies and reference books.

Read this example of non-fiction about Graffiti, then answer the questions on the next page.

Graffiti's Here, OK?

The *Oxford English Dictionary* defines graffiti as 'Drawings or writing scratched on a wall or other surface'. Taking this as a definition, people have been doing graffiti since the Stone Age when they etched drawings on cave walls. Today, graffiti surround us, and every school in Britain probably has some. Graffiti can be anything from initials carved into desks to rude scribbling scratched onto toilet walls for everyone to see. The word 'graffiti' is now also used to describe drawings, slogans or words created in public places with marker pens or paint. Are they art or vandalism?

Graffiti as art

Some modern day graffiti can certainly be called art, but what sort of graffiti do people think might improve our environment? *Most* people would probably say that graffiti can be called art when created in an *organised* way, for the enjoyment of those who are likely to see them. Examples of organised graffiti would be murals – walls carefully painted with pictures or patterns. But a *few* people say that some *unorganised* graffiti can also be called art. Exhibitions of 'unofficial' graffiti have been held at places like the Sought London Art Gallery in Peckham, and books about graffiti 'street art' have also been published.

Graffiti as vandalism

The people responsible for most graffiti are more interested in selfishly defacing our cities than in improving them. 'Tagging' is the ugliest form of graffiti – people write their personal 'signature' in public areas, sometimes even on historic buildings, with markers or spray paint. 'Tagging' started in New York, in America, in the 1970s but it has now spread to many European cities and London's Underground has become a big target. It is a crime, and the 'taggers' face great dangers. Some have been killed by falling onto live railway lines. 'Tagging' is costing Britain hundreds of millions of pounds a year to clean up – money that could be used to improve our environment in other ways and make our country a more attractive place to live in.

Questions

Use the information in the passage to answer these questions. Try to use your own words as far as possible.

1   When and where did 'tagging' start?

2   How do most people think of organised graffiti?

3   What does 'graffiti' mean?

4   What are the difficulties which face 'taggers'?

5   What is the main target for 'tagging' in Britain?

6   Where might you find an exhibition of 'unofficial' graffiti?

Activities

Now you are going to look at how the article tries to persuade readers that some forms of graffiti are art but that tagging is a form of pollution.

Imagine that this large piece of graffiti has appeared, overnight, on a wall in your school. Your headteacher wants it removed. Some of the teachers disagree.

1   What ideas can you find in the text which would help your headteacher to argue that the graffiti should be removed?

2   What ideas can you find in the text which would help you to argue that space should be set aside in your school for people to practise graffiti?

If the text you are looking at is a mixture of words and pictures, you need to:

- find your way around the text quickly
- respond to the way the text has been put together.

Reading an information text

Some texts, such as reference books, instructions or reports, are mainly concerned with giving information to readers. To make the material easier to understand the author may separate it out into different sections and use headings and illustrations.

When you only need *some* of the information in the text, it is useful to begin by gaining an overview of the whole text. Then you can find the parts you need to study in detail.

Finding your way around an information text

When you first look at the text you are trying to work out what is there. Ask yourself these three questions.

1 What do the headings tell me?

A headline or title should give some clues about the subject of the text beneath it.

2 What is in the main text?

You can use the method on page 10 to help you find this out.

3 What do the illustrations and captions show me?

Illustrations are usually placed on the page in a way that is designed to grab your attention. What they show will fit in with the ideas in the text.

Look at any drawings, photographs, charts or diagrams and think about:

- what each illustration contains
- what its caption tells you
- what any labels are pointing out.

ONE SPECIAL DAY

Most festivals are held over and over again, once a year or perhaps just once every ten years. But some festivals take place only once. They may commemorate an anniversary, such as 500 years since the founding of a particular city, or some great event in history. Spectacular ceremonies may be held at the coronation of a king or a queen or when someone becomes president. Special postage stamps are often issued to commemorate these events that fall outside the normal calendar of festivals.

A new century is always marked by public celebrations. And the start of a new millennium, as in the year 2000, deserves a very special festival indeed.

A NEW GERMANY

On 3 October 1990, Germany became a united country again. Since 1949 it had been divided into two separate nations, the German Democratic Republic and the Federal Republic of Germany. Crowds gathered to celebrate in the centre of Berlin.

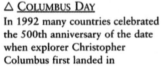

△ COLUMBUS DAY

In 1992 many countries celebrated the 500th anniversary of the date when explorer Christopher Columbus first landed in the Americas.

▷ AFRICAN CORONATION

Throughout the world, royal births, coronations, weddings or funerals are marked by glittering processions, splendid religious ceremonies and vast public gatherings. At his coronation, the ruler of Ghana's Asante people appears before his people wearing priceless gold ornaments and shaded by a ceremonial umbrella.

16

Questions

1   a   What does the main heading suggest the text will be about?
    b   What does the main text explain?
    c   How has the page been organised to help you find different pieces of information?
    d   Why do you think each of the illustrations was included?

2   Try to find out the following pieces of information as quickly as you can using the pictures and captions to help you.
    a   When did Columbus discover America?
    b   Why did crowds gather in the centre of Berlin in 1990?
    c   At an Asante Coronation, what type of metal are the Coronation ornaments made of?
    d   How are royal funerals celebrated throughout the world?

3   Draw a table with three columns like the one below. *In your own words* explain what you have found out about the way coronations and anniversaries are celebrated. Make sure you read and comment on the main text and captions, and look at the illustrations.

	Coronations	Anniversaries
Main text		People celebrate …
Captions		
Pictures	Special clothes, crown are …	

Reading a media text

Newspaper articles, advertisements and leaflets have to gain their readers' attention very quickly. A lot of work goes into deciding how a text should be put together to make sure it has the greatest impact.

When you are reading a media text you need to think about how its presentation affects the reader.

Check-list for reading a media text

1 Headings

Think: How does the heading grab my attention and why does it make me want to read on?

Remember:
   a   A bigger heading will be more noticeable than a smaller one.
   b   The wording is important.
   • Is it jokey? If so, it may suggest that the text will be lighthearted.
   • Is it puzzling? People will read on to find out what it is about.
   • Is it serious? If so, it might suggest that the text is serious, too.
   • Does it shock or startle? We love to read things which astonish us.

2 Subheadings

These are used to break up the text. They work like headings to attract your attention. They can:
   • help you find your way around the text
   • draw your attention to a particular part of the text.

3 Illustrations

These include photographs, drawings and diagrams. When you look at illustrations, you should notice:
   a   The **size** of the picture.
   • The bigger an illustration is, the more noticeable it will be.
   b   The **position** of the picture on the page.
   • The top or middle is the first part of the text you see.
   • The bottom of the page has less impact.
   • Does it matter what the picture is next to?
   c   What the picture **shows.**
   • What is the picture making you notice?
   • How does this tie in with the text?

4 Captions

These are written under a picture. They may:
- tell you what is in the picture
- tell you what the author wants you to notice
- give extra information
- comment on the picture.

5 Text

When you look at what is written you should look at:
- what is said
- how it is said.

The choice of **words** and **details** will be very important.

6 The order in which information is given

Texts are carefully planned. You should look at how the most important information is brought to your attention by asking yourself:
- where is it?
- how does the information fit together?
- how does the information build up its impact?

7 Tone

The best way to work out the tone of a piece is to see what 'tone of voice' the writer has written it in. You are really looking at the writer's style and deciding what the overall effect is. For instance, is the tone:
- lighthearted?
- mocking?
- serious?

8 Appearance

Paragraphs, words and pictures are drawn to our attention if they are made to stand out against the rest of the text. This can be done by using different kinds of print, colour, shading, framing, etc.

Ask yourself why the author wanted to draw your attention to each feature highlighted in this way.

Reading a newspaper article

The newspaper article below has been labelled to point out the effect of some of the features on pages 17–18.

Heading: Humorous approach calling Heather 'Supergran'. This compares her to Superman and other Super Heroes.

HEATHER IS WPC SUPERGRAN

WPC Heather Fenny is daily transformed into a vulnerable pensioner

Photographs: Pictures are placed next to each other to highlight the difference between how young WPC Fenny looks in uniform and how she looks when she is disguised as an elderly person. It is hard to believe it is the same woman.

Caption: Tells you who the WPC is and uses the word 'vulnerable' because she is trying to look like someone a thief could mug.

Tone: The writer is taking a light-hearted approach with words like 'Pounding the beat puts years on ...' to create a puzzle which makes readers wonder how dressing up as a pensioner can be 'in the line of duty'. It encourages them to read on.

It's the old Bill out to bag purse thieves

Main heading: 'old Bill' is a nickname for the police. Using the word 'old' fits in with the story of how a young WPC is pretending to be old. The word 'bag' is slang for making an arrest, and using it plays on the idea of the thieves stealing purses.

POUNDING the beat puts years on WPC Heather Fenny, but it's all in the line of duty.

For the 34-year-old officer spends her day shuffling around Newcastle disguised as a pensioner in an effort to catch bag snatchers. Her shift begins at Tyne Tees TV studios where it takes two hours to transform her from a fresh-faced young mum into a doddering decoy.

Once on the street she must wait for a thug to be attracted by the 'soft target', and the tempting purse sticking out of her bag. Out of sight, a back-up team waits to pounce.

Officers say the city centre is a haven for young thieves preying on defenceless pensioners.

Stolen

Heather, a mother-of-two who has been in the force for three years, said: 'It's unusual, but it's worthwhile.

'It must be terrible for an elderly person to have their purse or bag stolen. If we can stop this I'm happy to put myself in their position.'

She is in constant touch with colleagues via a radio under her coat.

The operation is being extended with more officers getting the aging treatment.

No wonder they call them the old Bill.

Paragraph 2: Starts to explain the story in more detail. Tells you where it is happening, and why the police are doing this.

Subheading: Reinforces what the story is about and sounds dramatic.

A final jokey comment like the one in the title – using the nickname 'old Bill' for the police.

Bottom picture: Shows the WPC in action. She is shown near young people which highlights how old she looks. You can see the disguise is working because no one seems to notice her.

Under the disguise, 'granny' is ready for action

Caption: Putting the word 'granny' in inverted commas emphasises that she is not really old. Just the idea of a granny being 'ready for action' seems comical because a real one may be too frail.

Daily Mail

Now it's your turn

Look at this leaflet carefully. It was written to persuade people to give money to care for the homeless.

Using the check-list on pages 17–18 to help you, discuss the labelled parts of the leaflet and explain what effect each has. Write down your ideas.

a How does this heading attract your attention and make you think about giving?

b What information does each caption give you?

c What does this tell you about the charity?

With nowhere to live, on a freezing cold night, what would **YOU** give for these...

Shelter
THE NATIONAL CAMPAIGN FOR HOMELESS PEOPLE

Registered in London: 1038133.
Charity No: 263710.

£15 could help give a homeless person a bed throughout the coldest part of the winter

£15 could help us provide over 30 nourishing hot meals for people sleeping rough

£15 could help us provide warm clothing for someone facing winter on the streets

BPD/R

d How does each picture show you that your money would be used wisely?

e How do headings encourage readers to give straight away?

f How does this response form persuade readers to fill in the donation boxes?

g What effect does the photograph have?

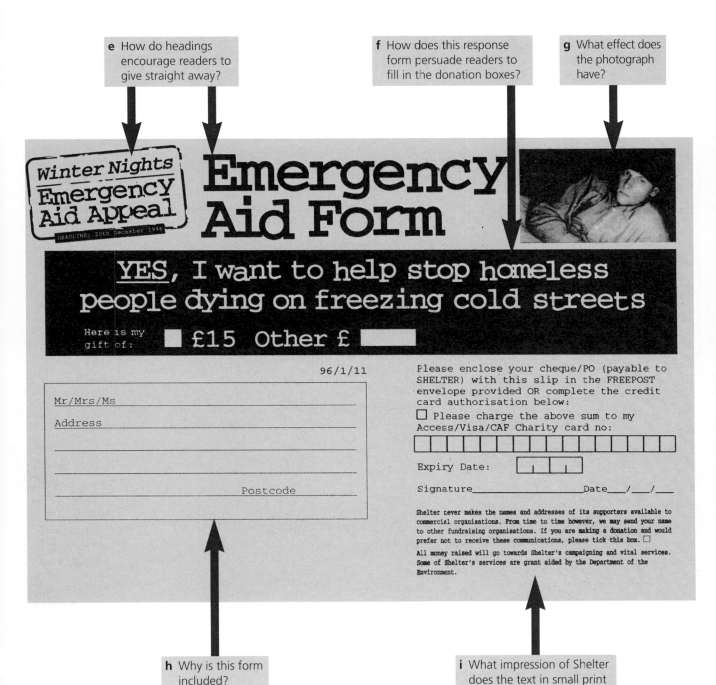

Winter Nights Emergency Aid Appeal
DEADLINE: 20th December 1996

Emergency Aid Form

YES, I want to help stop homeless people dying on freezing cold streets

Here is my gift of: ■ £15 Other £ ▭

96/1/11

Mr/Mrs/Ms _____

Address _____

_____

_____

Postcode _____

Please enclose your cheque/PO (payable to SHELTER) with this slip in the FREEPOST envelope provided OR complete the credit card authorisation below:

☐ Please charge the above sum to my Access/Visa/CAF Charity card no:

▭▭▭▭▭▭▭▭▭▭▭▭▭▭▭▭▭▭▭

Expiry Date: ▭▭

Signature _____ Date ___/___/___

Shelter never makes the names and addresses of its supporters available to commercial organisations. From time to time however, we may send your name to other fundraising organisations. If you are making a donation and would prefer not to receive these communications, please tick this box. ☐

All money raised will go towards Shelter's campaigning and vital services. Some of Shelter's services are grant aided by the Department of the Environment.

h Why is this form included?

i What impression of Shelter does the text in small print give the reader?

Reading an advertisement

Advertisements are a special kind of media text. When you study one, begin by working out these five things.

1	The **advertiser**	Look for a logo, name, address, or a well known slogan or image.
2	The **audience**	These are the people the advertisement is meant to reach. What information can you work out about them, for example: age group, interests, life-style, wealth, background, etc.?
3	The **purpose**	An advertisement might try to make you buy something, do something, or believe something.
4	What the **message** is	This is what the advertisement is telling you. For instance, the message could be about the product ('These are the best trainers you can buy'), or what the product will do for you ('This will make you really desirable').
5	How it **appeals** to you	Most advertisements appeal to a desire or feeling, such as: the desire to be popular or to win, our worries or fears, our sense of compassion, our respect for experts or our sense of humour. Advertisements usually suggest that their product will give readers just what they are looking for.

Your turn

Look at the advertisements on the next page. For each one, explain how you know the answers to these questions.

1   Who is the advertiser?

2   Who are the intended audience?

3   What is the purpose of the advertisement?

4   What is the advertisement's message?

5   What is its appeal?

Advertisement 1

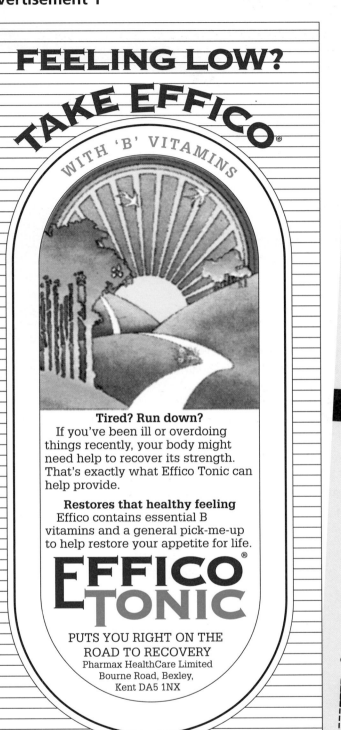

FEELING LOW?
TAKE EFFICO

WITH 'B' VITAMINS

Tired? Run down?
If you've been ill or overdoing things recently, your body might need help to recover its strength. That's exactly what Effico Tonic can help provide.

Restores that healthy feeling
Effico contains essential B vitamins and a general pick-me-up to help restore your appetite for life.

EFFICO®
TONIC

PUTS YOU RIGHT ON THE ROAD TO RECOVERY
Pharmax HealthCare Limited
Bourne Road, Bexley,
Kent DA5 1NX

FROM BOOTS, LLOYDS CHEMISTS AND CHEMISTS EVERYWHERE

ALWAYS READ THE LABEL

Advertisement 2

I'll be your best friend

Will you be mine?

Sponsor a dog for £1 a week and you'll have a friend for life ...
That's right, for just £1 a week you can sponsor an abandoned dog like me. You'll be helping the National Canine Defence League to give me, or another dog who may never be re-homed, a safe and happy life at one of its rescue centres. You'll also help the NCDL to care for other needy dogs. In return, you'll get a sponsor's certificate, updates on your dog – and a very faithful friend.

YES, I'd love a best friend

☐ Please send me my FREE poster guide so I can choose a dog to sponsor today.

Mr/Mrs/Miss/Ms/Other

Address

Postcode

Please return this form to: Sponsor a Dog, NCDL, FREEPOST WD360, 17 Wakley Street, London EC1B 1NA. Registered Charity Number 227523.   DS21

NCDL
National Canine Defence League
A Dog is for Life

Looking at details

Once you have gained a broad picture of what a text is about, read it through again to look at the details. Apart from making a piece more interesting to read, the details:

- give you more information about what something is like
- help create an impression of a person, place or thing
- help you notice differences
- may persuade you to do something.

Details create an impression

Read the following passage through quickly, then read it again thoroughly.

For a number of years Alan Bennett allowed an eccentric old lady, Miss S., to live in a van parked on his drive. This is what he wrote about her in his diary.

> *June 1980.*
>
> Miss S. has gone into her summer rig:
> a raincoat turned inside out, with brown
> canvas panels and a large label declaring it
> the Emerald Weatherproof. This is topped off
> with a lavender chiffon scarf tied round a sun
> visor made from an old cornflakes packet.
> She asks me to do her some shopping.
> 'I want a small packet of Eno's, some milk and
> some jelly babies. The jelly babies aren't
> urgent. Oh and, Mr Bennett, could you get
> me one of those little bottles of whisky?
> I believe Bell's is very good. I don't drink it –
> I just use it to rub on.'

Writing Home by Alan Bennett

You could respond to the passage very quickly by saying it just 'shows how odd Miss S. is'. However, to get the most out of what the author has written, you need to look at the details he has chosen to include and explain:

- **what** the details show about Miss S.
- **how** the details show that her oddness is special.

We have learned two important things about Miss S. in this passage:

- what she is wearing
- what she says.

Use the following questions to see how these details are used to help you understand Miss S. better.

Questions

1 **What is she wearing?**

Divide your page into three columns, set out like the table below. Make a note of each detail mentioned and try to explain what it reveals about Miss S. An example has been done for you.

What she wears	How she wears it	What this shows
a raincoat	turned inside out	It won't keep her as dry like this, so perhaps she's the sort of person who doesn't realise, or doesn't care about getting wet or about how odd it looks.

2 **What does she say?**
   a Make a list of everything Miss S. asks for. Explain what each item shows about her.
   b Now look at the list as a whole. What impression does it create?
   c Why do you think she says:
   - 'I <u>believe</u> Bell's is very good.'?
   - 'I don't drink it – I just use it to rub on.'?

Details can be used to persuade you

Advertisements must be able to persuade people who look at them for only a brief amount of time. Details in advertisements are chosen very carefully to create the greatest impact. When you look at an advertisement, these details may be in the pictures as well as the words.

Activity

1   Look at the advertisement for Acorn stairlifts. How does this advertisement try to persuade an elderly person to buy a stairlift? How have the details been used in this advertisement?

2   Look at the British Heart Foundation advertisement. How does this advertisement try to persuade adults to take part in the fundraising event? Pick out the details that have been used.

We'll fit one tomorrow. Straight up.

Call us now on freefone

0800 19 19 19

For a <u>free</u> no obligation quote.
- Next day installation available nationwide.
- Buy direct from the manufacturer.
- Thousands of satisfied customers.
- New or reconditioned.

ACORN STAIRLIFTS

GIVE YOUR LIFE A LIFT

 Remember

For each detail that you find, ask:
- What does it tell you?
- How does it help to persuade you?

THE **ISRAEL & JORDAN** EXPERIENCES

BRITISH HEART FOUNDATION

Top fund raiser?

Win a 4 day holiday for two in rural France

the **experience** of a **lifetime!**

Is a challenging and exciting bike ride around Israel or Jordan for you?

If so, read on:

Join us in 1997: 5–13 April or 12–20 April in Israel or 4–12 October in Jordan. Cycle 225 miles (4/5 cycling days) over a 9-day fundraising adventure.

Imagine cycling through deserts, craters and nature parks, past mountains and crusader castles, beside rivers, springs and seas. Depending on the itinerary chosen, you can cross the Sea of Galilee, float in the Dead Sea, cross the Negev Desert and visit Jerusalem, Petra, Eilat or Aqaba.

If you are reasonably fit, over 18, willing and able to raise sponsor money for the British Heart Foundation, then we want you.

Call today as places are limited. FreeCall 0500 200 575

British Heart Foundation
The heart research charity
Registered Charity No 225971

For more information, join one of our informal gatherings in Manchester (18 Sept), Glasgow (2 Oct) or London (9 Oct) – call British Heart Foundation National Events Department on 0171 487 7149

Activity

Read the two short articles written by different charities, below.

Using only the information you are given here, decide which charity you would most like to donate to. Explain how you made your choice.

You may find it helpful to work like this:

Step 1 Work out what each charity does.

Step 2 Look at the details included in each text.

Step 3 Think about what the details show you about the work of the charity.

The Dystonia Society

SOME people can't stop their heads jerking to one side; some can't stop blinking or open their eyes when they want to; some find that one of their hands has spasms so they can't write, play musical instruments or games as easily as they once could; some find that their voices are beyond control and that they can't speak audibly.

People with problems of this type are quite likely to be suffering from a form of DYSTONIA. This is a **neurological** condition which is thought to be very common but which few doctors are at present able to diagnose. Treatments are now available and are increasingly successful, some sufferers are able to lead normal lives again.

There is a vigorous society called THE DYSTONIA SOCIETY which exists to spread information about the condition and to help sufferers in any way it can.

neurological: *it affects nerves and muscles*

Talking Newspapers for the Blind

SUDDEN blindness in middle age left Fred devastated. Walking outside, crossing a road now took courage. Unable to watch TV, read newspapers or magazines, he faced isolation.

'Never mind, you can always listen to the radio,' said his well-wishers. It was not the same. Fred missed reading *The Independent*. Its regular features and columns were not on radio. Kind offers to read to him were not always convenient to Fred, until he was told of the Talking Newspapers Association UK.

TNAUK, a national charity, reads more than 180 national publications onto ordinary cassette tape for visually handicapped people. A million and a half tapes a year go out. Fred is now among 260 visually handicapped recipients of *The Independent* weekly digest on tape.

Besides weekly digests of daily and Sunday newspapers, there's a wide variety of national magazines on tape. Thousands with impaired sight are less fortunate than Fred. Nobody told them of TNAUK tapes.

A5 Is that a fact?

When you are reading a text, you often need to spot whether the detail you are reading is a fact or an opinion.

 ## Remember

A simple way to remember the difference:

Facts can be checked and proved.

For example: Chong is taller than Mark.
Richard drove from Dover to London last Sunday.

Opinions are what someone believes.

For example: My mum makes the best chocolate cake.
Linford Christie is the greatest athlete this country has ever produced.

Can you believe it?

When someone is arguing for their point of view they may make opinions sound like facts. Look at what people are saying here, and decide which are facts, and which are opinions pretending to be facts.

Everyone knows that girls are more caring than boys.

Casualty was so full on Saturday that we had to open another ward.

Good vegetarian meals are so tasty you won't miss eating meat.

More drivers received parking tickets from me today than ever before.

Activity

Most pieces of persuasive writing are a mixture of facts and opinions.

1   Read the passage below and find three opinions. Explain how each works to persuade the reader that a holiday in Ochra would be enjoyable.

2   Now, using only the facts, decide how well this holiday resort would suit each member of the Green family.

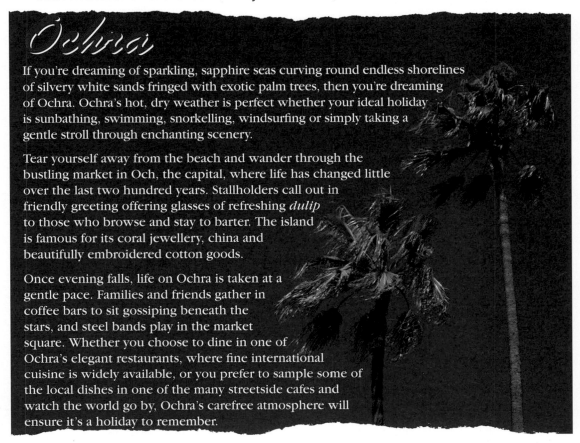

Ochra

If you're dreaming of sparkling, sapphire seas curving round endless shorelines of silvery white sands fringed with exotic palm trees, then you're dreaming of Ochra. Ochra's hot, dry weather is perfect whether your ideal holiday is sunbathing, swimming, snorkelling, windsurfing or simply taking a gentle stroll through enchanting scenery.

Tear yourself away from the beach and wander through the bustling market in Och, the capital, where life has changed little over the last two hundred years. Stallholders call out in friendly greeting offering glasses of refreshing *dulip* to those who browse and stay to barter. The island is famous for its coral jewellery, china and beautifully embroidered cotton goods.

Once evening falls, life on Ochra is taken at a gentle pace. Families and friends gather in coffee bars to sit gossiping beneath the stars, and steel bands play in the market square. Whether you choose to dine in one of Ochra's elegant restaurants, where fine international cuisine is widely available, or you prefer to sample some of the local dishes in one of the many streetside cafes and watch the world go by, Ochra's carefree atmosphere will ensure it's a holiday to remember.

Meet the Green family

Dianne Green would like clean, sandy beaches for her daughter to play on. She is looking forward to a good rest and the chance to paint some landscapes. Dianne particularly enjoys bartering in markets for local souvenirs.

Mark Green is a sports fanatic but suffers from sunstroke if he spends too long out in the sun. Mark particularly enjoys finding out about different types of music played around the world.

David Green's idea of a good holiday is windsurfing and discos. He wants to get a good tan while on holiday. David is fanatical about computers and would like to go somewhere where there are Cyber cafes so he can surf the Internet.

Tina Green is seven and, while she likes swimming and playing on the beach, her idea of heaven is going on funfair rides. She enjoys eating outdoors as this lets her watch other people as they wander past.

Bias

Presenting information so that it fits in with a particular point of view is called **bias**. Bias is created by choosing which facts and opinions are told, rather than telling everything in a balanced way.

Remember

Only giving one side of the story in a piece of writing has a powerful effect on readers. Biased texts often appear very convincing. This can cause problems because they are usually written to persuade a reader to agree with the writer's point of view.

Some examples of biased writing are easy to spot, others are more subtle.

- The narrator of a story may be biased against an enemy and only tell you bad things about that person.
- A leaflet arguing that a local beauty spot should be protected against developers will only tell you one side of the story.

Activity

The following articles have been written about the same person, but from two very different points of view. Read them carefully, then answer the questions.

A

Last week's lottery winner, local man Michael Sterling, has lost no time in splashing out.

Already he has made a generous donation to St Stephen's premature baby care unit.

'It was the least I could do,' Mike said, 'I can't bear the thought of a lack of money meaning vital equipment isn't available when someone's baby really needs it.'

Impulsively generous, as soon as Mike realised he had won millions he rushed down to his local pub, The Fox and Hounds, to celebrate with his mates, telling them, 'The drinks are on me.'

Cheryl, Mike's wife of thirty years, is already sporting a dazzling new eternity ring which makes up for the heartbreak she suffered earlier in the year when the first one Mike gave her was stolen. Mike also plans to take Cheryl away for a romantic break to Devon where they have so many happy memories of their honeymoon.

'While we're there we'll talk about what to do with the cash,' said Mike, who loves his £15 000 a year job so much he doesn't want to leave it. 'I'd hate to think the money will change me in any way,' he explained.

But Mike admits he's thinking of getting rid of his battered D reg Astra and buying a new car. 'We'll have to see if we can afford it,' he jokes.

B

'I'd hate to think that the money will change me in any way,' says local lottery winner Mike Sterling.

The problem is, mean Mike means it!

On the night of his win he waited till nearly closing time at The Fox and Hounds, before turning up to buy his mates a single round of drinks, and, despite winning millions, has so far only given a tiny fraction away to charity.

Mike's nearest and dearest isn't doing too well either. Sporting a half crescent eternity ring which finally replaces the one the burglars took earlier in the year, Cheryl, his faithful wife of thirty years, knows there's no hope of a second honeymoon in Barbados. Mike is taking her away to Devon for a week, to 'talk about what to do with the cash.'

Whatever happens, Mike is determined to stay on at his £15 000 a year job and is regularly seen still driving around in his battered D reg Astra.

Won't he even be thinking of buying a new car?

'We'll have to see if we can afford it,' Mike says.

Questions

1   Make a list of any facts which are in both articles.

2   Which facts appear only in A, and which only in B?

3   Pick out three opinions from A, and three from B.

4   **a**   What kind of person does Mike seem to be in A?
  b   What kind of person does Mike seem to be in B?

Reading between the lines

Read the passage below, which is the beginning of a story.

Once there were three children called Lydia, Christopher and Natalie. Lydia was the oldest, Christopher was the middle child and the youngest was Natalie. Their parents were divorced and disliked each other. On the day that this story begins the children are going to visit their father, Daniel. Their mother has written Daniel a letter and told the children to give it to him.

Questions

1 What have you learned about this family?

2 Do you think this is a good way to begin a story?

3 Does this passage make you want to read on?

4 Does it grab your attention?

Now read the beginning of Anne Fine's book, *Madame Doubtfire*.

Madame Doubtfire

All the way up the stairs, the children fought not to carry the envelope. Towards the top, Lydia took advantage of her height to force it down Christopher's jumper. Christopher pulled it out and tried to thrust it into Natalie's hand.

'Here, Natty,' he said. 'Give this to Dad.'

5 Natalie shook her head so violently her hair whipped her cheeks pink. She interlaced her fingers behind her back. So Christopher tucked the envelope down the top of her pinafore dress, behind the yellow felt ducklings. Natalie's eyes filled with tears, and by the time Daniel Hilliard opened the door to let his children in, she was weeping gently.

10 He reached down to pick her up in his arms.

'Why do you always have to make her cry?' he asked the other two.

Lydia looked away. Christopher blushed.

'Sorry,' they said.

Daniel carried Natalie through the hall into the kitchen and sat her on 15 the edge of the table. Hearing a soft crumpling of paper inside her dress, he reached in behind the yellow felt ducklings, and pulled out the letter.

'Aha!' he cried. 'Another missive from The Poisoned Pen. How *is* your mother, anyway?'

'Very well, thank you,' Lydia informed him with slightly chilly courtesy.

20   'I'm very glad to hear it,' he said. 'I wouldn't like to think of her going down with amoebic dysentery, or salmonella, or shingles.' His eyes began to glitter. A little smile warped his lips. 'Or Lassa fever, or rabies, or –'

     'She had the beginnings of a slight cold last week,' Lydia interrupted her father. 'But it never took off.'

25   'Pity,' said Daniel. 'I mean, what a pity.'

Madame Doubtfire by Anne Fine

Readers are really detectives …

Did you notice that the two passages are about the same characters in the same situation? The difference is that in the second version, instead of just *telling* you what is going on, the author has *shown* it to you. Then she has left you to work out what the facts are, and to make sense of the relationships and the family's situation from the hints and clues that she has placed in the text.

- Usually writers *show* rather than *tell* their readers what is going on, because this makes their work more interesting to read. It also means that to get the most out of a text, readers need to become detectives.

- Readers need to pick up clues from details such as a character's appearance, expressions and behaviour. Then they need to ask: What do these say about the person?

- When you read a text, work out how the characters feel about each other from what they say or think and how they treat each other. Think about what an author's choice of words is suggesting about a place or a person.

What clues can you find?

Using the passage from *Madame Doubtfire,* how do you work out that:

1   Lydia is the oldest child and Natalie is the youngest?

2   It is their mother who has written a letter to Daniel?

3   The parents do not get on?

What else can you discover?

Look at the passage from *Madame Doubtfire* again.

1   What do the details in lines 1–11 show you about how the children get on together?

2   What do the details in lines 17–25 show you about how Daniel feels about his ex-wife?

3   Looking closely at the whole of the passage, work out how the children feel about the relationship between their parents.

Remember

When you write about what you have found, always include evidence from the text (words, phrases and ideas) to show that what you are saying is true.

Be alert

Looking carefully at the **details** when you re-read a piece of writing is a good habit to get into with any text.

Read the following newspaper article carefully, then answer the questions.

It's lawn and disorder for hedgehog orphans

LUCK: Baby hedgehogs find a safe refuge from the killer cutters in the back gardens   Picture: DOUGLAS MORRISON

by REBECCA HOLMES

LIFE has become far too prickly for these baby hedgehogs. For they have all been orphaned by a new enemy – the common or garden lawn strimmer.

It seems the whirring flexible cutters are killing off their mothers, leaving them with little hope of survival. Unless, that is, they are taken to the Farthing Wood Wildlife Hospital at Cobham in Surrey.

Peter Walder, the manager there, has received at least 45 over the last few weeks. But he is baffled as to why the problem has become worse this year.

'Perhaps people are leaving their grass to get longer and so don't see the family of hedgehogs hiding in the undergrowth,' he said yesterday.

'All we can imagine is that more people are using hi-tech strimmers rather than the old-fashioned lawn mowers.

'It is very distressing, all these babies are wandering around screaming for their mothers. We are asking all gardeners to be extra careful.

'Go through the long grass gently with a stick and make sure there are no creatures there.'

The babies will be hand-reared until the autumn when they will be released back into the wild.

Daily Express

Questions

1 How does the writer want us to respond to the baby hedgehogs' problem?

2 How does the writer view the work done by the Farthing Wood Wildlife Hospital?

Make sure you explain which details help you work out the answers to these questions.

Reading poetry

Poems can be some of the most exciting and rewarding texts to read – if you will let them. It is easy to dismiss a poem as 'too difficult' simply because you did not understand it all the first time you read it. You need to give yourself (and the poem) a chance. Any poem deserves to be read several times. Read it so you can hear each word. Listen to it. Enjoy it.

Do not worry if there are parts of it you cannot quite work out! You will be able to unravel it further by reading it thoughtfully and thoroughly. The rest of this unit shows you how to do this. Start by reading the following poem through several times.

Steam Shovel

The dinosaurs are not all dead.
I saw one raise its iron head
To watch me walking down the road
Beyond our house today.
5   Its jaws were dripping with a load
Of earth and grass that it had cropped
It must have heard me where I stopped,
Snorted white steam my way,
And stretched its long neck out to see,
10 And chewed, and grinned quite amiably.

by Charles Malam

Now copy the poem out carefully, placing it in the centre of a new page of your work book.

Make sure that you leave a lot of space all around the poem, so that you can make notes as you study the poem in more detail.

1 Thinking about what the poem says

Start by asking yourself 'What does the title tell me?'

Next, if the poem has punctuation, read it sentence by sentence and try to work out roughly what is going on.

If there is no punctuation then read the poem aloud (or in your head) and stop where you have to pause for it to make sense. Then look back at the part you have just read and try to work out what it is about.

> **What is the poem *Steam Shovel* about?**
>
> In your own words, very simply, make a note <u>at the bottom</u> of your copy of the poem about what you understand about the poem.
>
> Your answer might start like this:
>
> *The poem is called 'Steam Shovel' which helps you work out what the monster is …*

What if the poem is more difficult than this one?

If a poem seems very complicated you may need to:
- change words round in a sentence
- put the sentences in a different order until they make sense.

2 Finding the ideas

The poem will probably have started to make some kind of sense to you by now. To understand more of what it is about, ask yourself questions such as:
- what is the poet really looking at?
- is it something outside himself?
- is it something inside himself?
- what is he trying to make me think about?

> **Carry on working on the poem *Steam Shovel* but this time write your answers to these questions in the space <u>above</u> the poem.**
>
> Make sure that you:
> - **explain** what you think the poet is making you think about
> - **prove** that your ideas are sensible by referring to what is in the poem.
>
> The following sentences should help you get started:
>
> *The poet is looking at a machine called a steam shovel and describing it using a surprising picture – he compares it to a dinosaur. This makes us look at the machine in a new way, and we have to think about …*

What if I have to read a longer poem?

Keep on asking yourself these questions while you are reading because there is more room in a longer poem for changes of ideas.

3 Looking at the way the poem is written

Once you have a fairly clear idea of what the poet is trying to say, it is time to think about:

- **how** the poet has chosen to write the poem
- **how** these choices affect the poem.

Make sure you look for:

a   any details, words, phrases or lines which stand out while you are reading the poem

b   any patterns – rhymes, rhythms or repetitions – you can spot

c   the way the poem is set out on the page.

> **Now make notes round your copy of *Steam Shovel*.**
>
> Label any details you notice, and jot down the thoughts you have about the poem.
>
> The example below will give you some ideas of how to do this:
>
> compares modern — The <u>dinosaurs</u> are not all dead. — surprising start!
> machine to a   I saw one raise its <u>iron</u> head —   can't be a real
> prehistoric monster.   To watch me …   dinosaur + iron
> Why?   is very strong.

Be careful …

If you know any technical terms and spot examples of them in a poem you are studying, take care!

There is no point in just saying 'the poet has used alliteration/imagery/assonance/onamatopoeia'. You must be able to say what effect the words used in that way have in the poem.

4 Thinking about 'feelings'

Although this can seem quite hard to pin down, a feeling, overall mood or impression may be an important part of the poem.

When you read, look out for:

- the overall mood
- the tone it is written in (tone is explained on page 18)
- any emotions expressed or experienced
- any impressions that you notice.

> Think about *Steam Shovel*, looking especially closely at lines 5–10 as you try to answer this question:
> - What impression of the machine do you gain in these lines? Make sure you explain which details gave you this impression.

Activity

Now it is your turn to work through a poem by yourself.

 Remember

1 Read through the poem slowly several times so you can hear it.

2 Read the questions you will have to answer.

3 Finally, when you read the poem **thoroughly and thoughtfully,** jot down any thoughts you have about the poem.

Old Mister Roberts

Old Mister Roberts lives on the corner
next to the sweetshop. Tall and dusty,
very slow moving; walks with a cane.
Thin dry face, all stretched and bony,
5 straight pinched nose with bristly whiskers,
not much hair, but bushy eyebrows,
small blue eyes as bright as flames.

Old Mister Roberts goes out walking;
raises his hat if you say Good Morning,
10 shakes his stick if you call him names.
Always wears an old red waistcoat,
jacket patched with leather elbows,
wears no collar when it's sunny,
wears a trilby when it rains.

15 Old Mister Roberts was a sailor:
round the world with coal and timber
– probably sailed the Spanish Main.
Sometimes, in the park in Summer,
you can meet him when he's walking;
20 then he'll sit and tell you stories,
dreaming that he's young again.

by Tony Charles

Questions

1 What is the poem about?

2 Pick out five words or phrases that have a particular effect on you. Explain why you think they work well in this poem.

3 **a** What impression do you gain of Mister Roberts?
  b Which details give you this impression?

A8 Dealing with difficult words

If a piece of writing is hard to understand, it is usually because:

- some of the words are new to you
- words you usually understand are being used in a new way
- the ideas in it are strange to you
- the sentences are difficult to read.

To start dealing with a problem text you need to decide what it is that is so hard – for example, is it just some of the words, or the whole thing?

Using a dictionary

Look up the exact meaning of a difficult word in a dictionary. Then try to put it in your own words so that the explanation you have found makes sense in the sentence you are reading.

Once you make a habit of using a dictionary, you will get to know the meaning of many more words. After a while you will find there are fewer unfamiliar words for you to look up when you are reading a new text.

Activity

Read the following passage through, using a dictionary to help you understand the exact meaning of the words in **bold** type.

Then, **in your own words**, explain what each of them means.

Sending an unsigned Valentine card can be a **hazardous** business.

First you have to **purchase** the card without being spotted. Then, if you're not going to sign your name, you have to find some other way to **convey** something about who you are. Otherwise your **beloved** may think your card was sent by someone else.

Even when you've solved that problem, **dispatching** the card isn't easy either. Postmarks can be too much of a clue, and delivering it yourself is **fraught** with difficulty.

Of course, you can always ask a friend to help you out of the **predicament** by writing the card, addressing it for you and even delivering it – but it's not nearly as much fun.

Without using a dictionary

What do you do if you do not have a dictionary or the definition you find does not seem to be much help? There should be enough clues in the text to help you work out the meaning of any word you are stuck on.

Use what you do know, to work out what you don't know

First, you need to understand roughly what the sentence containing the word is about. You can work this out by asking yourself these three questions:

1 What is the whole passage about?

2 What is the paragraph containing the difficult word about?

3 What is the sentence containing the difficult word about?

Next, look at how the difficult word fits into its sentence. Try to explain what the word must mean if it is going to make sense in that sentence. The explanation you give is likely to be the meaning of that word.

Activity

Each of these passages has a word printed in **bold** type. Try to understand the general meaning of the passage to help you work out the meaning of that word. Then write a definition of what each word in bold means within its sentence.

1 The teacher explained, 'When you're answering the questions on Act I of *Romeo and Juliet*, use the **explanatory** notes that are printed at the side of each speech. They should help you work out what is going on.'

2 Computer technology is changing so fast that by the end of this year most of the machines in this room will be **obsolete**. Then we will have to buy new ones.

3 When Peter started the new job, he thought people had seemed pleased that at last here was someone who 'stuck by his guns'. Slowly as the weeks went by he began to notice a change. Unable to back down or to admit that he had made a mistake, Peter's **obdurate** nature was making him unpopular.

4 At the first sign of snow our cat always finds a warm spot to curl up in. She hates getting wet and cold. When shooed out into the snow for some exercise she hovers by the back door miaowing loudly. If the door is opened, even a crack, she darts back along the winding passageways, and in and out of rooms, until at last she finds some other cosy **nook**.

5 Once you looked at the carpet more closely you could tell that the weaving was **inexpert.** Uneven rows and snapped off threads told their story. The maker was only an apprentice.

Do you know the meaning of a word that is similar?

If you look closely at the word you do not understand you may see that it resembles, or is made up of, other words whose meaning you *do* know. This, together with knowing what the sentence is about, can help you guess the meaning of a difficult word.

Activity

In each of the sentences below the word in **bold** type belongs to a family of words. Using the definition of what another member of the word family means to help you, explain what the words in bold type mean.

1 The cake was made of **alternant** layers of chocolate sponge and vanilla ice cream.

an **alternative**: one of two or more possibilities.

2 I can't stand **braggarts** – you should let other people sing your praises.

to **brag**: to boast.

3 My father runs a **haulage** company.

to **haul**: to drag or pull.

4 The bouncer gave Jake a **quizzical** look when he walked into the nightclub wearing only a dinner jacket and shorts.

a **quiz**: a test where questions are asked to test knowledge.

5 The area of Horby had been **popularised** by the television series *Castles in the Air*.

popular: to be well known and liked.

6 At least when they got there, the **hostel** would be warm and dry. How Anne longed for this journey through lashing rain to end!

a **host**: a person who has invited guests to visit, and then looks after them during their stay.

A9 Writing about texts

You are rarely asked only to read a text. More often than not you have to write about it. As there is so much to say about anything you read, make sure that you can show what you know.

When answering questions, think about the following points.

What does the question ask for?

Unless you answer the question that is actually there on the page, much of what you write will be wasted. Read through a question several times and work out exactly what it wants you to do before you begin looking for the answer.

Remember

1 If the question asks you to refer only to a certain part of the text, do not write about ideas that come from somewhere else.

2 Look at *how* the question wants you to write about the material. For example, you may be told to use your own words.

3 If the question suggests specific areas you should look at in your answer, then take care to include them.

Be thorough

Make sure that you give enough details in your answer.

Go through the relevant part of the passage sentence by sentence, picking out everything you can.

Prove your point

Make sure that you show that you have a good reason for making a point.

Do this by referring to the text to show where you got your answers. The answer below gives you an example of how to refer to the text.

Question: What does Anna feel when her mother says 'No'?

Answer: When her mother says 'No', Anna is angry. **She stamps her foot and throws down the tea towel**.

The words in **bold** are details taken from the text to prove that Anna is angry.

Use quotations

Copying a few words out of the text and putting them in your answer is called **quoting**.

If you are going to quote a piece of the text to prove your point, you should:

- pick out the **shortest** piece of text which will help you make your point – this should be only a few words or a single sentence
- set out the quotation with **inverted commas** around the whole piece of text you are quoting, like this:

Anna
'… stamped her foot and flung the tea towel down …'

Remember

1 When you copy a word or phrase from the text, make sure you:
   - copy exactly
   - put the word or phrase inside quotation marks.

2 If a quotation is more than three words long it needs to be set out on a new line.

3 If the quotation is not a whole sentence you should show which parts are missing by using three dots (this is called an **ellipsis**).

4 If the quotation is taken from a poem you must set it out on your page to look exactly the same, line by line, as the poet has set it out in the poem.

Explain how your quotation proves your point

There is no point in quoting from a passage unless you explain to your reader what you want them to notice in the quotation.

You could explain your ideas something like this:

The words 'stamped' and 'flung' show how angry Anna is because they sound forceful.

Always write in clear, well organised English

As you want the person marking your work to know that you have understood what you have read, it is important that you make your work easy for them to read.

These rules should help you to do this.

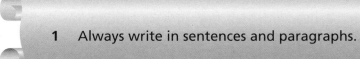

1   Always write in sentences and paragraphs.

2   Think about your spelling, grammar and punctuation as you write.

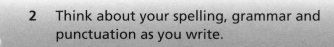

3   Organise what you say to make it clear that you are actually answering the questions asked, and not just 'waffling on'.

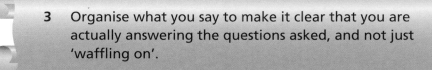

4   Read your answer through after you have finished writing and make sure that it makes sense.

B1

A silver lining

Sam's mother, Isabel, owns a second-hand dress shop. A stranger has just given her a pile of old clothes among which they discover a fur coat with something hidden in the lining. Now Sam, her mother and her brother Seb, must go to a wedding. Granny has offered to look after the shop while they are away.

In the bus, Seb said to our mother, 'Now don't tell Father about the money if he *is* there.'

He did turn up. He was his usual 'charming' self, never stuck for words. I was pleased enough to see him to begin with, but after a bit when I saw him
5   sweet-talking our mother and her cheeks beginning to turn pink and her eyes lighting up, I felt myself going off him. Seb and I sat side by side and drank as much fizzy wine as we could get hold of and listened to her laugh floating down the room.

'She'll tell him,' said Seb gloomily.

10   She did, of course. And he decided to come home with her. They walked in front of us, holding hands.

'When will she ever learn?' said Seb, sounding strangely like our granny.

'Good evening, Torquil,' said that lady very stiffly, when we came into the shop where she was sitting playing Clock Patience on the counter top.
15   'Stranger,' she couldn't resist adding.

'Hi, Ma!' He gave her a smacking kiss on the cheek. 'It's good to see you. You're not looking a day older.'

She did not return the compliment.

'Been busy?' asked my mother.

20   'Not exactly rushed off my feet. I sold two or three dresses and one of those tatty Victorian nightgowns – oh, and yon moth-eaten fur coat in the cupboard at the back.'

She might just as well have struck us all down with a sledgehammer. We were in a state of total collapse for at least five minutes until my mother
25   managed to get back the use of her tongue.

'You sold *that* coat?'

'Well, why not? You hate having fur lying around.'

'Who did you sell it to?' My mother was doing her best to stay calm.

'How should I know? Some woman. She came in asking if we had any furs.
30 She gave me twenty pounds for it. I didn't think you could ask a penny more.
Lucky to get that.'

My mother told my granny about the money in the lining and then it was
her turn to collapse. I thought we were going to have to call a doctor to revive
her. My father managed it with some brandy that he had in his coat pocket.

35 'Oh no,' she moaned, 'oh *no*. But what did you leave it in the shop for,
Isabel?'

'It was in the back shop! In the cupboard.'

They started to argue, to blame one another. Seb and I went out and
roamed the streets till dark and long after, looking for the woman in our fur
40 coat. We never did see it again.

Our father left the next morning.

'Shows him up for what he is, doesn't it?' said our granny. 'He only came
back for the money. He'd have taken you to the cleaners, Isabel. Maybe it was
just as well. As I always say – ' She stopped.

45 Not even she had the nerve to look my mother in the eye and say that
every cloud has its silver lining.

Rags and Riches *by Joan Lingard*

Questions

1   **a**   How does the family travel to the wedding?
    b   Who does the family meet at the wedding?
    c   What has Granny sold?
    d   What did the fur coat contain?

2   **a**   How does Sam feel about her father?
    b   What does Seb realise about his mother at the wedding?
    c   How does Granny react to Torquil when she first sees him?
    d   What good does Granny think has come out of the disaster?
    e   What kind of person is Mother? Explain how you know.

 Key points

Make sure you know what a question is asking you to do before you start writing your answer.

1   To get good marks when answering questions like question 1 above, you need to:
    • find the right information in the text
    • write about it in complete sentences.

2   To give good answers to questions like question 2 above you must do a lot more. You need to:
    • find the places in the text which you think provide evidence for your answer
    • read those parts of the passage thoroughly and thoughtfully
    • look for the details which help you work out your answer
    • write your answers in complete sentences, making sure you refer to the text and explain what all those details show.

For example, for 2c, one of the details you could include is the use of the word 'stiffly' (line 13). Part of your answer might be:

Even though Granny politely says 'Good evening, Torquil' the word 'stiffly' lets you know that she does not really want to be friendly. She is not rude, but she wants him to know she does not approve of him.

B2 Face to face

All Frankie wanted to do was try to grow her own monster. The rest of her family were brilliant scientists so surely she should be able to do something as simple as that?

Unfortunately the monster she makes soon looks like it is dead. Feeling rather disappointed, Frankie leaves it in her empty fish tank and goes to bed for the night.

Next morning she wakes suddenly to find there is a face next to hers on the pillow …

I shot out of bed so fast that I must have broken the sound barrier. When I opened my mouth and screamed, no sound came out.

I stood with my back to the window. I was trapped. It was between me and the door.

5 The monster sat on the pillow and stared at me with its red eyes. It had changed again. It was now – most horribly, grotesquely – half human in shape. It had a domed head, but no hair, no nose, no ears. It had two eyes and a thin slit of a mouth, as if someone had drawn a line in soft clay with a knife; a thick body, short stumpy arms and legs. But no hands or feet. Its
10 grey flesh had a greenish tinge. It looked absurdly like a very large jelly-baby.

'Go away!' I shouted. My voice cracked and crackled in my throat like cornflakes. I stamped on the floor and shook my fist at it threateningly.

It scuttled off the bed, across the carpet and hid under the table. The lid had come off the **aquarium** and was lying on the floor, upside down.
15 It crouched behind it, but it was too big. Its bottom stuck up in the air and it trembled.

I took a step towards the door but my knees gave way and I collapsed on to the bed. I sat there, with my legs tucked under me, trying to recover my strength. I was afraid I was going to faint.

20 The monster peeped at me from behind the lid and ducked down again. It did this three times, and then, emboldened perhaps because I did not move, it came out from behind its barrier, crawling on all fours like a baby.

'Go away!' I shouted, waving my arms.

It scuttled back immediately, falling into the lid in its hurry, so that its
25 stupid short legs stuck up into the air.

aquarium: a tank in which you keep pets that need to live in water

I laughed. I expect I was hysterical. Or mad. I can't think of any other reason why I didn't scream and run from the room like any sane person would have done. I just sat on my bed and watched it.

30 It was playing now. It sat in the upside-down lid as if in a boat, and rocked backwards and forwards until the lid tilted too far and tumbled it on to the floor. It seemed to enjoy this for it did it several times.

Then it looked at me. Its eyes were very round and a clear light crimson. Quite a pretty colour, really. It began twisting its slit of a mouth in the most ridiculous manner. Now it would bend the corners down until it looked like a
35 croquet hoop; now up into a capital U. Once it even managed to twist it into a figure eight. I couldn't help laughing at it. It didn't seem to know what a mouth was for. It never opened it, not once. Perhaps it wasn't a proper mouth at all.

Now it stood up and started stretching its legs. I don't mean the way we
40 stretch them, but like elastic. Its fat, short stumps grew longer and thinner until they couldn't bear the weight of its body and it fell down. Its legs shrank back to their previous size and it sat up and looked at them and then at me, as if puzzled.

I laughed again.

45 Someone knocked at my door.

'Don't come in!' I shouted, and the monster scuttled back under the table again and hid. It seemed surprisingly timid for a monster.

The Monster Garden by *Vivien Alcock*

Questions

1 What does Frankie do when she first sees the monster?

2 How does the monster try to hide itself when Frankie tells it to go away?

3 Copy and then fill in the rest of this table to show in which ways the monster looks human, and in which ways it does not.

Looks human	Does not look human
It has a domed head. It has two eyes.	It has not got …

4 What is the first thing that happens which makes Frankie laugh?

5 In your own words, explain all the different ways the monster uses the aquarium lid.

6 What does Frankie like about the monster's face?

7 Why do you think Frankie shouts 'Don't come in!' (line 46) when someone knocks on her door?

8 How do you know that Frankie is scared when she first sees the monster?

9 How do you know that the monster is scared when Frankie shouts at it?

10 How do Frankie's feelings *slowly change* during the passage? You should be able to spot at least four changes.

Remember

1 You will need to look for single words or phrases in the text to help you to explain your answers to this type of question.

2 Look at page 43 for help on how to quote words or phrases from the passage in your answer.

Key points

Sometimes a writer tells you exactly what a character is feeling. At other times, as in this story, you have to work out what the characters are feeling from the clues the writer gives you.

You can find out what a character is feeling by looking at:

- **what they do:** when Frankie stamps her foot she is trying to be brave.
- **what they say:** Frankie shouts 'Go away!' because she is frightened.
- **what they think:** later on, when Frankie starts to like the monster, she even notices how pretty its eyes are.

Read the poem below and then answer the questions that follow.

Biking free

Black tyres spin –
pattern's tread –
spokes flicker –
legs of lead.

5 Steel rim squeals –
brake blocks clasp –
squeeze as hard –
as a bully's grasp.

Streets blur by –
10 eyeball stings –
handles gleam –
cycle sings.

Pounding pulse –
heart beats' race –
15 clicking gears –
furious pace.

by Pie Corbett

Questions

1 Make a list of all the bicycle parts mentioned in the poem.

2 Which line tells you where the bicycle is being ridden?

3 Which words or phrases (small groups of words) show you that cycling is hard work?

4 Which words or phrases show you that the poet is enjoying the bike ride?

5 Look at the second stanza. How does this image (word picture) make you think about how hard the rider has to apply the brakes?

6 How has the poet made you aware of how fast the bike is travelling?

Remember

Do not just think about what a poem says, the **way** that it says it matters too.

 Help

To answer this question properly you need to hear the poem again, as well as to look at how it is written on the page. While you are doing this try to notice these things:

lines and stanzas
- are they long and slow to read?
- are they short and quick?

rhythm
- is there a regular or an irregular beat?
- is it quick or slow?

punctuation
- where does each sentence start and end?
- what effect does this have?
- why do you think the poet has used a dash at the end of most lines?

 Key points

1 Studying a poem means looking carefully at a number of things, including the way it is built. More often than not a poem is made up of **lines** which are grouped in **stanzas**, but it may also have other patterns helping to hold it together.

2 The words the poet has used may have been chosen because their **sounds create a pattern**. This is one of the reasons why listening to a poem is important. Hearing it more than once is a good way of helping you notice what effect any strong rhythms or rhymes have.

3 Just looking at how two words are spelt is not always enough to remind you that they rhyme. After all, think about 'bough' and 'cow'.

B4 In the queue

The following extract is taken from a book by Blake Morrison about the life of his father. It describes a time when the family are stuck in a traffic queue.

A hot September Saturday in 1959, and we are stationary in Cheshire. Ahead of us, a queue of cars stretches out of sight around the corner. We haven't moved for ten minutes. Everyone has turned their engines off, and now my father does so too. In the sudden silence we can hear the distant
5 whinge of what must be the first race of the afternoon, a ten-lap event for saloon cars. In an hour the drivers will be warming up for the main event, the Gold Cup – Graham Hill, Jack Brabham, Roy Salvadori, Stirling Moss.

My father does not like waiting in queues. He is used to patients waiting in queues to see him, but he is not used to waiting in queues himself. A
10 queue, to him, means a man being denied the right to be where he wants to be at a time of his own choosing, which is at the front, now. Ten minutes have passed. What is happening up ahead? What fathead has caused this snarl-up? Why are no cars coming the other way? Has there been an accident? Why are there no police to sort it out? Every two minutes or so my father gets out
15 of the car, crosses to the opposite verge and tries to see if there is movement up ahead. There isn't. He gets back in and steams some more.

In the cars ahead and behind, people are laughing, eating sandwiches, drinking from beer bottles, enjoying the weather, settling into the familiar indignity of waiting-to-get-to-the-front. But my father is not like them. There
20 are only two things on his mind; the invisible head of the queue and, not unrelated, the other half of the country lane, tantalizingly empty.

And When Did You Last See Your Father? *by Blake Morrison*

Questions

1   A first paragraph often sets the scene. What do you learn from the opening paragraph here to help answer the questions, 'When?' and 'Where?'?

2   The second paragraph here concentrates on Blake Morrison's father. What clues are given about his job?

3   Keep looking at the second paragraph. What impression do you get of what his father is like?

4   There are five questions in the second paragraph. Find them. How do they help to build up a sense of what is going on?

5   Look at the first sentence of the third paragraph. Describe in your own words how these other people are behaving.

6   Why do you think Blake Morrison describes the people in the other cars?

7   What do you think is the most effective part of this whole description? Explain your choice.

 Key points

In this passage Blake Morrison is setting the scene.

- **Scene-setting** is descriptive writing that prepares the way for what is going to happen. Some people think that descriptive writing simply means describing everything you can see. That is not usually true. Details will normally be selected to help give a particular impression.

  In this case, the details are helping you to build up an impression of Blake Morrison's father and of the tension created in his father by the traffic jam.

- **The first paragraph** helps to set the scene generally. When the car's engine is turned off, the family can hear the motor racing actually starting, which helps to emphasise how they are stuck when they would all like to be somewhere further up the road.

- **The second paragraph** concentrates on father. The word 'queue' turns up four times in the first few lines, which emphasises what the problem is. Then there are the five questions. The sheer number of questions that his father is asking highlights his frustration. He does not really want answers, he just wants the traffic to move.

- **The third paragraph** offers a contrast. Not all drivers are behaving like Blake's father. This paragraph also suggests what his father is thinking.

Oh, and just in case you never read the whole book, his father *did* pull out around all the other cars and drive on the wrong side of the road to the front of the queue.

B5 The 2-minute call …

The leaflet on pages 57–60 is from Help the Aged. It describes how SeniorLink line came to the rescue when Vera Smith had a bad fall. Read the leaflet and then answer the questions below.

Questions

Look at the front of the leaflet (page 57).

1 How does the picture help the message of the headline and of the leaflet?

 Help

Think about what would be lost if you had no picture.

Look at the middle of the leaflet (pages 58 and 59).

2 Look at lines 1–5. What happened to Vera Smith?

3 Why do you think the sentence in line 4 is underlined?

4 Look at what Lyn, the SeniorLink operator, says. How does she try to keep Vera calm?

5 Look at what Vera says. What is there to suggest that she starts to panic?

Look at the back of the leaflet (page 60).

6 Do you think the headline is a good one or a bad one? Give reasons for your opinion.

7 Look at the two stories under the words <u>Some cases are particularly tragic</u> (lines 37–43). Why do you think these cases have been chosen?

8 Look at the words that have been printed in **bold** type in lines 31, 44–46, and 58–59. Why do you think they have been picked out in this way?

9 Choose one other phrase or sentence that you would pick out in **bold** type. Say why you chose it.

Now read the Key points about advertising on page 61.

THE 2-MINUTE CALL THAT SAVED HER LIFE...

'If it hadn't been for the voice at the end of the SeniorLink line, I could have died'. Mrs Vera Smith, Woking

Below, you'll see the record of an actual telephone call that took place between Vera Smith, an elderly woman, aged 87 and Lyn Barker, an operator at the SeniorLink response centre. It all happened after Vera, who lived alone, slipped and fell on her kitchen floor when she was preparing

5 breakfast. To her horror, she found she was unable to get up again. Grasping the SeniorLink alarm pendant which was hanging around her neck, she hurriedly pressed the response button ...

Vera

Lyn, SeniorLink operator

Lyn Good morning, Mrs Smith, Lyn speaking, how can I help you?

Vera Please ... help me!

Lyn All right Mrs Smith, I hear you. Have you hurt yourself?

10 **Vera** I ... I don't know. My legs ache and ... I can't get up.

Lyn Stay calm Mrs Smith, I'll ring your neighbour, Mrs Fisher, and ask her to come and help you.

OPERATOR PUTS MRS SMITH ON HOLD AND CALLS NEIGHBOUR

Lyn   Mrs Smith, your neighbour is not answering. Are your front and back doors locked?

Vera   I think so . . . please help me . . . now there's a burning smell in the kitchen . . .

15   **Lyn**   It's all right Mrs Smith, I'm going to call someone to help you.

OPERATOR PUTS MRS SMITH ON HOLD AND SUMMONS THE FIRE BRIGADE

Lyn   Mrs Smith, help is on its way. Don't worry.

Vera   Please hurry! There's black smoke coming from the grill!

Lyn   All right, I'm going to call someone else to help you.

OPERATOR PUTS MRS SMITH ON HOLD AND SUMMONS BOTH POLICE AND AMBULANCE

20   **Lyn**   Mrs Smith, help will be with you any second.

Vera   Please hurry! I can't move and I'm scared!

Within just 2 minutes of Mrs Smith calling, Lyn had alerted the police, fire and ambulance services.

25   **Lyn stayed on the line, reassuring Vera until the police arrived some minutes later. As they forced their way in to rescue her, thick black smoke was filling the kitchen.**

THE SENIORLINK CALL HAD SAVED HER LIFE.

VERA IS ALIVE AND WELL – BECAUSE SHE COULD HEAR VOICES.

Mrs Smith was fortunate enough to have a
SeniorLink telephone in her home. And you'll be glad
to know she made a full recovery from her ordeal.

30

But many other elderly people aren't so lucky.

In fact, every week in Britain, between 300 and 500
isolated elderly people die alone and unnoticed in
their homes. Often, neighbours don't even notice

35 there is something wrong.

Some cases are particularly tragic.

One elderly man's body was only discovered when
the appearance of swarms of flies inside his glazed
front door alerted a neighbour.

40 In another case, council workmen boarded up the
flat of an elderly man while his body was still inside.
No one could be sure whether he had been alive
when the boarding up work started.

Yet tragedy <u>can</u> be avoided in cases like these.
45 **All it takes is for isolated elderly people to
hear voices.**

Please give to our appeal and help us <u>stop</u> isolation
killing elderly people in Britain. Help us fill their lives
with friendly, caring, <u>life-saving voices.</u>

50 SeniorLink is one of the most effective ways for
isolated elderly people to hear potentially life-saving
voices.

Essentially, it is a specially designed telephone system
that uses a small transmitter, worn as a pendant or

55 bracelet, enabling the wearer to summon help
wherever they are.

It gives vulnerable elderly people like Mrs Smith
confidence in knowing that they are **never
completely alone.**

Help the Aged

Registered Charity No. 272786

Key points

1. Advertising is about getting the message across. Help the Aged clearly want their supporters to know how they are spending their money. The messages about SeniorLink are:
   - it works well
   - it stops tragedies.

2. To reinforce their message, the charity has taken a real-life example. The sense that this is something that actually happened is helped by several things:
   - the picture of the person saved
   - her name, age and where she lives
   - the words of the actual call which saved her life.

3. Advertisers know that they have to work hard to keep your attention – that is why they avoid great chunks of writing. In their efforts to keep your interest and get across their message they use a range of devices:
   - headlines
   - pictures
   - quotes in large print
   - words underlined
   - words in bold type
   - words in capitals.

   These things help to make the message reader-friendly. They are also there to help you notice the basic message of the advertisement. This means that you can still pick up the key points, even if you miss some of the detail.

Diary of a survivor aged 8½

Christian Aid is a charity that raises money to help people in developing countries. In the following advertisement, eight-and-a-half-year-old Madan Ram describes his life in a carpet factory. Read the whole of the advertisement before you start answering the questions on page 64.

DIARY OF A SURVIVOR AGED 8½

April Paro talked today and the boss lashed her with the cane. He shouted at us 'if you children speak you are not
20 giving your whole attention to the product'.

May My fingers bled again and the boss got angry with me for getting blood on the loom. He says I will
25 work extra hours for the next two days and I will be fined and that will increase my father's debt to him. I cried when he talked about Papa.

June The boy who lost a hand, poor
30 Rangilal, he fainted today. We begged the boss to open the window. 'The mud walls are hot sir. The thermometer says 105 sir'. But the window stays shut to keep out the insects that eat the wool.

35 **July** Not much light gets through the polythene slats in the roof. It's hard to see the pattern. I made mistakes today and I'm frightened what will happen when the boss finds out.

February I don't know why I am here. I think my Papa sold me to the boss to learn a trade and now the boss says I must do exactly what he
5 tells me.

March It's the same every day. We go from our beds to the loom at six. No one must talk. We tie tiny knots all day, the smallest ones on the
10 carpet because we have small fingers. Work, work, work. My fingers crack and weep and sometimes my eyes get all blurred. We get a cup of dahl and half an hour to rest then go back to
15 the loom till night time. There is no more food. We are too tired to play.

40 **August** In bed tonight, Nageshwar told me his plan to escape. He is brave but he is bigger than me. He said we live worse than animals because an animal can roam when it is hungry.

45 **September** There is a big welt on my arm where I was whipped yesterday for falling asleep at the loom.

October The boss says we are behind on the carpet. We are too slow. So 50 instead of starting at six we will start at four. And instead of stopping at eight we will stop at 11. Three boys are crying but I feel too tired to cry.

November A big commotion today. 55 Nageshwar and his two younger brothers escaped.

December Nageshwar is back and we have been told that the same thing will happen to us if we try to 60 escape. He has been branded with hot iron rods.

January I want to study, I want to be a teacher, and when I grow up I will earn money and help my father out of 65 his debt. That's what I want to do, if I get out of here.

This diary is based on interviews with Madan Ram and other children recently working in carpet 70 factories in Uttar Pradesh, India.

These children have been rehabilitated with the help of Christian Aid, but in India alone an estimated 15 million children still 75 spend their entire childhoods slaving in bonded labour to help their parents out of debt.

Christian Aid works to fight child labour in countries throughout the 80 Third World. We can't do this without your help. Please give all you can in Christian Aid Week.

- -

Questions

1 Read the diary entry for February again. How does Madan Ram believe he came to work in a carpet factory?

2 Read the entry for March. What evidence is there that Madan Ram's health is suffering in the factory?

3 Read the paragraphs for April and May. Find an example of the cruelty of those who run the factory.

4 Read the entry for June. How can we tell that the carpets matter more than the children?

5 Read the diary for July and August. Why does one boy think animals have a better life than they do?

6 Read the entries for September and October. What hours are the children now working?

7 Read the diary entries for November, December and January. How do the factory bosses try to make sure that there are no more escapes?

8 Read lines 67–82 of the advertisement. What is Christian Aid trying to do?

9 Look at the advertisement as a whole. Choose two things about this advertisement that you think make it work well. Say why you have chosen them.

Remember

- When you are giving an opinion, you need to **explain** why you hold that opinion.

- Reasons that are clear to you, need to be made clear to others.

1 Information in advertisements is always broken down in some way to make it more readable. Here it is done by presenting the story month by month. The questions have followed that month-by-month pattern.

2 Sometimes you will be given a single longer question. It might look like this.

> **How does this advertisement develop a sense of horror about children's lives in these illegal carpet factories?**

- If you are asked that sort of question, you will need to think harder than you did here about how to organise yourself. Look for the natural divisions in the material you are studying. Here it is the monthly diary entries. In another text, it might simply be the different paragraphs.

- It also helps to think about how the question could be broken down into smaller parts. There are lots of things about the horror of the carpet factories in this advertisement. They can be broken down into at least two main parts:

  a the working conditions
  b horrifying incidents.

  Dividing things up like this makes it clearer what you are looking for.

3 When you are sorting out your ideas, you will often need to make a note of what you find. Making notes can save you time because you are less likely to get confused. You are also more likely to collect together all the information you need, which will mean higher marks.

4 In an examination or a test, it can be helpful to underline or highlight the parts you want to use. If you are looking for more than one sort of information, use more than one colour.

B7 The Cockatrices

If you thought you saw a dinosaur, would you believe your eyes? Well, when the people in this passage see a Cockatrice running towards them they have a real problem in persuading others that they are telling the truth.

On a dark freezing December evening a truck driver called Sam Dwindle burst into his foreman's office looking very upset. He was white and sweating, and he shivered badly despite the thick jacket he wore.

'Yeah, yeah, I know just what you're going to say,' he told the boss.
5 'But listen to this: an hour ago when I was coming up the A3 from Portsmouth, on that new bit of bypass, I see this *Thing*, with big three-cornered flaps along its back and a tail the length of a tennis court and round ears that swivelled about like radar shields, and it was running along beside the motorway on its four fat legs.
10 Running as fast as I was driving! And I was doing seventy –'

'Then you didn't ought to of been,' said his boss, 'not with a load of wine glasses. I suppose you'd put in a couple of hours at the George in Milford?'

'No, I hadn't, then,' said the driver, injured. 'I knew you
15 wouldn't believe me. And if you don't, I'm sure I don't care. But I'm telling you, if that *Thing* had taken a fancy to cross the A3, instead of going off Dorking way, your truck would have been as flat as a Brillo pad and me with it. It had a **tassel** on its tail,' he added. 'And flaps there too!'

20 'And a bow of pink ribbon on its head, I suppose,' said his boss.

'OK, OK! You can give me my cards. If there's going to be things like that around, I'm going back to window cleaning.'

The next of the Cockatrices was sighted by a school **botany** class, who were out on the moor near the town of Appleby-under-
25 Scar, two hundred miles to the north of the first occurrence. They were hunting for rabbit and deer tracks in the snow.

Two boys, Fred and Colin, had run on ahead of the rest, but they came racing back to the main group as fast as their legs would carry them. 'Miss! Come and see! There's a dinosaur in
30 Hawes Dell.'

tassel: a tuft, or a fringed end

'Now what moonshine have you got in your heads?' remarked the teacher, Miss Frobisher. But the whole class hurried up to the lip of the **dell** and looked down into it.

'Gracious me! Somebody must be making a film,' said Miss Frobisher. 'But
35 that's not an *ordinary* dinosaur, Colin. It's a, it's, um, Tyrannosaurus Rex. You can tell that from its teeth and claws. The claws are at least eight inches long, and the teeth –'

'Will it bite us?' nervously asked a girl called Lily.

'No, dear. It's only a model, a very clever one indeed. I wonder where the
40 cameramen are, and the film technicians. Dear me, what a lot it must have cost to make a model that size.'

'It's coming this way,' said Fred.

'Coo, it doesn't half stink,' said Colin. 'Like a whole truckload of rotting seaweed. Are you sure it's only a model, Miss?'

45   'Now Colin! Use your intelligence! You know there aren't any dinosaurs about any more. They lived millions of years ago.'

'Look at its tracks in the snow,' said Lily. 'Aren't they huge? Listen to it pant. Miss, I'm scared. I want to go home.'

'Don't be a baby, Lily,' said the teacher. 'Just when you've got a
50 chance to study this very clever model, which must be radio-controlled. Now you can see what it would have been like to live millions of years ago –' Those were her last words.

The newspapers carried the story of the mysterious disappearance of Miss Frobisher and her class. 'Their tracks
55 were traced as far as the top of Hawes Dell,' reported the *Appleby Herald*, 'but heavy snow falling soon after prevented the police from discovering where they had gone after that. A local farmer, James Robson, claims to have seen what he described as a
60 "mammoth footprint" in the snow, but there has been no confirmation of his suggestion that some large beast was responsible for the strange **fatality**. Mr Adrian Mardle, Chief Constable of West Humberland, is
65 in charge of the case.'

The Cockatrice Boys by Joan Aiken

> **dell:** *a hollow with trees in it*
> **fatality:** *death*

Questions

In this unit you are asked to answer only two questions. You will need to answer both questions in a lot of detail.

1 What do you learn about the monsters in this passage? Make sure you use your own words as much as possible in your answer.

 Help

You will find it easier to write a good answer if you look through the passage and find:

- what the monsters look like
- how the smell of the monsters is described
- what the monsters do
- how the monsters move
- what people say about them
- what people feel about them.

2 The passage tells you about two sightings of the Cockatrices. Which sighting did you find most entertaining, and why?

 Help

The two sightings of a Cockatrice are quite different. To help you compare them, copy the chart below and fill in all the details. When you write your answer, make sure you explain *how* any of the details you picked out added to your enjoyment of the story.

Remember

In a comprehension you need to:

1 **Quickly read through the whole text** to grasp what it is about.

2 **Read the questions** so you know what you have to find out.

3 Then **read the passage again** noting the parts you will need to study closely to find the answers.

4 Read those parts of the text again **thoroughly and thoughtfully** to work out the best answers.

Details		First sighting	Second sighting
1	Where it took place	on the A3	in Hawes Dell at Appleby-under-Scar
2	Who saw it		
3	How they reacted		
4	Any funny things said		
5	How the monster was behaving when it was seen		
6	What happened to the people who saw the monster		
7	How the people who did not see the monster reacted to the sighting		
8	Any other details you enjoyed		

Key points

It is not just what happens in a story that makes it enjoyable. The way it is told matters too.

1   When you **read thoroughly** look out for details such as:

• interesting names	e.g. *in Hawes Dell at Appleby-under-Scar*
• vivid descriptions	e.g. the way the terrible smell of the Cockatrice is described as: *Like a whole truckload of rotting seaweed …*
• how people speak	e.g. *'Now what moonshine have you got in your heads?'* remarked *Miss Frobisher …*
• what people feel	e.g. *Sam Dwindle … looking very upset. He was white and sweating, and he shivered badly despite the thick jacket he wore.*
• what people think	e.g. Miss Frobisher thinks the monster is only a model and then it eats her!

2   Then read the details you have picked out thoughtfully and try to understand
   • why you noticed them
   • what they add to the text.

B8 Animal refuge

The following article is one of a series of reports published in *The Independent Magazine* which looked at the different lives of six young people. They described not only what they did and how much money they had to spend but also how they felt about their lives.

Animal refuge

Sarah Marshall, *14, lives with her sister and parents in the Suffolk village of Newbourn, and attends the local school for girls. She receives £5 a week pocket money for clearing horse manure from the fields. Her mother works for Ipswich council, her father is*
5 *a civilian worker in the police force. She owns her own horse and breeds gerbils.*

'Being 14 can be horrible. Adults ignore your opinions,' says Sarah. 'There was this time when I went into hospital to
10 have a mole removed, and the doctor spent the whole time explaining it to my mother. He didn't look at me once. I wanted to scream, "Talk to me – I'm the one having the operation".'

15 Her bedroom is neat and tidy. 'My grandma cleaned it before you arrived,' she admits candidly. 'Normally, you would find left-over Pot Noodle containers and curry plates under the
20 bed, and *Smash Hits* magazines, records and art work over the floor for my parents to trip over.' Posters of her favourite bands adorn the walls: Oasis, Blur, Boyzone and her particular
25 favourites, PJ and Duncan. She hasn't got a boyfriend: 'They tend to see me as a friend and call me "mate".'

She is allowed to go out once a week to the Rollerink, but she must be home
30 by 11 pm. 'I'm sure my parents don't let me go out with much money because they're worried about me spending it on alcohol or cigarettes or worse, though I wouldn't. I know people who smoke and
35 drink, some who say take drugs, but I don't. My parents would be hysterical.'

She has a strawberry-roan horse called Rumple, and just today has taken delivery of a bigger mare called Cat, a present from
40 her parents. Her last big present before this was a bike worth £130, for her birthday. 'When I feel down,' she says, 'I go for a ride on my horse to the river and think.' Or she goes to her caravan at the back of her
45 house, where she keeps gerbils. 'The caravan is my real place to escape. Many people don't realise how intelligent gerbils are; they can fall in love with each other.'

The caravan has a shabby old sofa and
50 old chairs, and smells, predictably, of
sawdust and gerbils. There is no television:
'The gerbils wouldn't like TV.'

There is a phrase among today's
teenagers: 'social meltdown'. It
55 represents the shame and scorn that
adolescents pour on their peers who do
not conform to their brand-name/
designer dress code. Sarah knows all
about social meltdown: 'My family
60 isn't poor, but we're not as well off as
some of the girls at school. Some of
them get £50 a month pocket money,
and extra for clothes. They think it's
important to have Lee or Levi jeans and
65 Reebok sports gear, but I don't. I often
shop in charity shops.'

'I used to be painfully shy. I let it
crush me. Then one day I thought,
"This cannot go on, I have got to try
70 and be myself," and I began to
open out.'

Sometimes the other girls call her a
misfit. 'They used to sing this song by
Pulp called "Misshapes" every time I
75 walked into the classroom. I went out
and bought the record and decided I
liked the words. Still, it will probably
always remind me of school.'

Question

1 What do you learn about how Sarah thinks and feels from this article?
Use the questions below to help you find the material you need to
do this.

 Help

Answer these questions in note form. Remember that you are going to
use your notes to answer the main question. Make sure you can follow
what you write down.

   a   What does Sarah think about the hospital doctor?
   b   How does Sarah think boys respond to her?
   c   How does Sarah think her parents feel about her?
   d   What are her feelings about smoking, drinking and drugs?
   e   How does horse-riding help Sarah?
   f   How does Sarah feel about gerbils?
   g   What role does the caravan play in her life?
   h   How does Sarah feel about rich and not-so-rich teenagers?
   i   What does Sarah say about shyness?

Key points

1   There are plenty of **facts** in this article about Sarah Marshall's
    life. The questions you have just answered have concentrated on
    opinions and emotions. It is often quite easy to see the
    difference between facts and opinions. Take this sentence:

    She owns her own horse and breeds gerbils.

    No one is going to mistake those two facts for opinions.

2   In other parts of the article, you might need to think more
    carefully. Sarah says that she does not take drugs because her
    parents would react hysterically. Her choice about drugs is
    presented as being a fact about her life. Her view on how her
    parents would react is an opinion. It may be one hundred per
    cent accurate but it is still only her view.

3   Facts and opinions are often interlinked in an article but it is
    quite common to find more of the facts at the start of an article
    and more of the opinions towards the end. This is the case in
    Sarah Marshall's story: indeed, the whole of the first paragraph
    is factual.

4   Sometimes you will be told where to find the information you
    need in a piece of writing. At other times you will be expected
    to go through it yourself and pick out the right parts. It is
    important not to get worried if you do not immediately find
    what you need in order to answer a question. Do not panic
    when whole sections are not relevant. Being able to ignore the
    parts you do **not** need is just as much a skill as finding what
    you **do** need.

B9 Goggle-eyes

Kitty has taken such a strong dislike to her mother's boyfriend, Gerald, that she calls him Goggle-eyes. One evening her mother and Gerald are out and Mrs Harrison (**Mrs H**) is babysitting. Kitty tells her sister Jude what she feels about Goggle-eyes and what she has written about him in her English homework.

Kitty Well, I don't like Goggle-eyes. Not one bit.

She waves the essay she's been writing in the air.

5 And everyone at school is going to know how much I hate him.

Jude Why? What's that?

Kitty It's just an essay. Called 'Something I Hate'.

10 **Jude** Kitty, that's mean.

Kitty jumps on a chair, and reads aloud.

Kitty 'Something I hate comes round to our house practically every day now. Slimy and creepy and revolting, it makes me absolutely sick. It walks
15 in here and acts as if it owns the place. The first thing it does is switch off all the lights it thinks we don't need. "There!" it says. "That should slow the little electric wheel down to a sprint!" Then it starts goggling at Mum, and telling her what to wear. And Mum's so wrapped up in this new thing of hers that she doesn't even notice that –'

20 *Kitty breaks off.*

What's that?

Jude What?

Kitty That noise.

Jude It's them. They're back!

 Remember

1 The way drama is set out on the page makes it seem much longer than prose, but do not let this put you off.

2 When you read a drama script you have to work out what characters are like from:
  • what they say
  • how they treat other characters
  • stage directions which show *how* they speak or behave
  • what other characters say about them
  • how other characters treat them.

25   *Jude snatches up her homework book and rushes to greet them. Hastily, Kitty slides her essay out of sight under a newspaper on the table. Gerald walks in, followed by Mum.*

Gerald   Hello, Kitty.

Kitty   *(sourly)* Hello again.

30 **Jude**   Mum! Look at this! I got a tick for all the homework Gerald did with me.

       Gerald walks round the room, switching off all the unnecessary lights.

Mum   That's wonderful, Jude! Well done!

35 **Gerald**   There! That should slow the little electric wheel down to a sprint.

       Kitty raises her eyes to heaven.

Mum   Did you hear that, Gerald? You and Jude have done very well indeed at school today.

40 **Gerald**   Oh, goody!

Kitty   Oh, for heaven's sake!

       Kitty turns away. Gerald shrugs his shoulders at her back, then whips out a box of chocolates.

Gerald   We've earned these, then, Jude.

45   *He walks across to Kitty.*

       Would you like one, Kitty?

Kitty		*(sourly)* No, thanks.
Jude		But they're your favourites, Kitty.
		Kitty narrows her eyes at Jude.
50	**Kitty**	I said, 'No, thanks!'
		Mrs Harrison wanders in.
	Mrs H	Ooh chocolates! Lovely.
	Gerald	Do have one, Mrs Harrison.
	Mrs H	I won't say no.
55	**Gerald**	In fact, have two. Have yours and Kitty's. She's not having any.
	Mrs H	Aren't you, dear? I thought these were your favourites.
		Kitty scowls horribly.
	Mrs H	Well, I won't say no. I'll have this one.
		She dithers endlessly.
60	**Mrs H**	And this one. No, this one. No, this one.
	Mum	I'll find my purse, and see you out.

Mum leaves the room. Mrs Harrison trails after her, busily unwrapping her chocolates. Gerald settles on the sofa, and Jude snuggles up beside him.

65	**Jude**	*(wheedling)* Read to me, Gerald.
	Kitty	*(imitating softly)* Read to me, Gerald. Pretty, pretty, please …

Jude gives Kitty a glare. Gerald reaches over to unfold a paper lying on the arm of the sofa.

70	**Gerald**	'Shares continued their steady revival today, with the FT Share Index finishing the week improving thirty-three points, to one thousand, seven hundred and fifty …

Jude's thumb creeps into her mouth, and she snuggles closer.

The FT 30 share index gained twenty-seven point three points to one thousand, four hundred and five, crossing the fourteen
75   hundred points line for the first time in two months. Gilts improved by up to three quarters of a million –'

Gerald breaks off suspiciously. He inspects the date on the top of the paper.

80   Hang on! I thought that all sounded a bit familiar. This is yesterday's paper. Where's today's?

Kitty moves forward quickly, but is too late. Gerald has reached across for the paper on the table. When he picks it up, Kitty's essay slides onto the floor.

Hello. What's this?

85   *Kitty bites her lip.*

Kitty   Nothing. Just a bit of rubbish. Don't bother with it. Just drop it in the bin.

Gerald is about to crumple it up when he notices the writing on it.

Gerald   No, I don't think so, Kitty. I think it's some of your homework.

90   **Kitty**   No, really! It's –

Gerald   No, listen.

He holds it up and reads.

'Something I hate comes round to our house practically every day now.

95   *Jude puts her head in her hands. Kitty hangs her head.*

Slimy and creepy and revolting, it makes me absolutely sick. It walks in here –

Gerald stops. He gives Kitty a glance. Then he reads on, in a cooler tone.

100   It walks in here and acts as if it owns the place. The first thing it does is switch off all the lights it thinks we don't need.

He stops again, looking astonished. When he reads on, it is in a tone of sheer wonder.

105   "There!" it says. "That should slow the little electric wheel down to a sprint!"'

He stops, and looks around at
all the lights that he switched off
earlier. Then he lowers the sheet of
110   *paper and looks reproachfully at
Kitty. Kitty stares back defiantly.*

Jude   *(bravely)* She didn't mean it, Gerald.

Gerald is still looking at Kitty.

Gerald   Oh, I think she did.

115 **Jude**   No, honestly. It was just a joke.

Gerald   A joke?

Jude   *(desperately)* Yes. A joke!

Mum comes back in, closing her purse.

Mum   A joke? Have I just missed a joke?

120   *There is a horrid silence. Then, suddenly, Gerald takes charge.*

Gerald   *(cheerfully)* That's right. You missed a joke.

Mum   What joke?

Kitty and Jude look nervously at Gerald.

Gerald   All right. I'll tell it again. What did the cannibal
125   with one leg say when they asked him if he'd enjoyed
his holiday?

Mum   I don't know. What did he say?

Gerald   He said, 'It was excellent. Apart from the fact that it was self-catering.'

130 **Mum**   *(laughing)* Oh, that's horrible!

Mum turns to Kitty and Jude, who are staring at Gerald in disbelief.

Don't you think it's funny?

Gerald casually crumples up Kitty's essay.

Gerald   You can't expect them to laugh, Rosalind. They've already heard it.

135   *He winks at Kitty, and drops the essay safely in the bin.*

Goggle-Eyes *by Anne Fine*

Questions

1   Why does Kitty dislike Gerald so much?

 Help

You should look at each of these different things in detail:
a   what Kitty has written in her essay
b   what Gerald does
c   how Gerald gets on with Mum and Jude.

2   How does the writer keep the audience's interest as the scene goes on?

 Help

Start by thinking about:
a   why it matters if Gerald or Mum read the essay
b   what happens to the essay during the scene
c   how Gerald tries to make himself popular with the girls
d   what you expect Gerald to do when Mum asks if she has missed a joke
e   what effect telling the lie and throwing the essay away may have on Kitty and Gerald's relationship.

Key points

Drama is often exciting when there is **conflict** – when there is some kind of struggle going on between two characters.

1   There has to be a good reason for the conflict, otherwise you will lose interest. You have to be made to believe the conflict really matters to both characters.

2   In the script you have just read, the conflict is between Kitty and Gerald. As the scene develops we learn that they want very different things:
    • Kitty does not like Gerald going out with her mother, she does not want Gerald around.
    • Gerald wants Kitty to accept that he is going out with her mother and to let him be part of the family.

3   Several times the conflict becomes stronger. One example is when Gerald hands round the chocolates, clearly hoping that this will help win Kitty over. The conflict becomes even stronger because Kitty will not accept chocolates from him, not even if they are her favourites.

4   When Kitty's essay falls into Gerald's hands there is more conflict because he finds out all the horrible things she thinks about him and starts to feel very angry. At this point Gerald has the chance to get his revenge. All he has to do is tell Mum what Kitty has written and she would get into a lot of trouble.

5   The conflict is overcome (for the moment) because Gerald decides not to tell Mum the truth. Instead he chooses to use the situation to try to win Kitty over by hiding what she has done. This is quite a surprise for Kitty and the audience; and surprises are always interesting.

B10 Anything for a laugh

While John Ryan, his best friend Gerry and his other friends have been waiting in the lunch queue, Neil Delaney has written *'Bluebottle on a bun'* in place of the words *'beefburger in a bun'* on the menu board. Mr Doyle, the headmaster, is annoyed, but having wiped off the graffiti he goes back to his office without having found out that it was Neil who had done it. John Ryan describes what happened next.

As he swept towards his office Phil gave a low whistle. 'I thought he'd go berserk,' he remarked.

'He would if somebody did it again,' said a voice behind us.

5 It was Neil Delaney, and for some reason he was staring pointedly at Gerry. We'd hardly spoken since the weekend and I was a bit put out to discover him in Neil's company.

'Go on, Ger,' urged Neil, producing a stick of chalk. 'Nobody's looking.'

Gerry's face went white.

'Not scared, are you?' sneered Neil.

10 Gerry looked around. Satisfied that the teachers and dinner ladies were busy, he crept over to the board. He thought for a moment or two then wrote in his spidery scrawl *Beefbangers make you burp*. I couldn't believe my eyes. Gerry used to do just about anything to keep out of trouble and here he was tweaking the tiger's tail.

15 'Yes?'

I looked up. Mrs McCartney the head dinner lady was tapping her ladle against an aluminium tray full to the brim with curry sauce. 'Burger on a bun or curry?' she asked.

'I don't know.' I was still staring at Gerry's handiwork.

20 Mrs McCartney's eyes followed mine. 'The cheeky little hounds!' she exclaimed. 'They've done it again.'

'Done what?' asked Neil innocently.

'You know what,' said Mrs McCartney. 'Did you do it?' she snapped, glaring at me. 'You look dead shifty, you do.'

25 'No,' I answered. 'Honest.'

She leaned across the counter. 'Mrs King, could I have a word?'

Our class teacher was stapling work to one of the display boards.

'Yes, what is it?' she asked pleasantly.

'That,' said Mrs McCartney. 'They've been messing with the board again.
30 And Mr Doyle has rubbed it off once.'

At the mention of Mr Doyle's name, the smile vanished from Mrs
King's face.

'I'll tell Mr Doyle,' she said, 'Keep these children here.'

As Mrs King went off in search of him, Mrs McCartney stood hand on hips,
35 swinging a ladle threateningly and glaring at us as if we'd just mugged a
nun. 'One of you has had it now,' she warned.

'Have you lost your marbles?' I asked Gerry.

'Shut up you!' he shot back irritably. I think he was getting worried.

'How do we get out of this one?' I demanded, ignoring him.

40 'Just keep your trap shut, Ryan,' Neil ordered, his eyes narrowing.

I didn't need telling twice. It was a case of shut your trap before I shut it for you. Just then Mrs King returned with Doyley.

'It was them lads,' said Mrs McCartney. 'I reckon it was that one.'

She was pointing straight at me.

45 'Now, now, Mrs McCartney,' said Doyley. 'You can't go accusing people without proof.'

I felt something, like a hand tugging at my trouser pocket. Neil reminding me to keep my trap shut, no doubt.

'I think we'd better go to my office,' Doyley continued.

50 As we trooped from the hall the whole school was completely silent.

'I don't suppose anyone would care to own up,' he said, closing the door. He supposed right. Everyone just stood shuffling their feet or staring fixedly at the carpet.

'Then you'd better empty your pockets,' he sighed.

55 He must have spotted the confused looks because he immediately added: 'I assume one of you still has the chalk.'

I couldn't avoid stealing a glance at Gerry. He was for it now.

'You first Neil,' said Doyley as pointedly as he could. Neil duly laid his belongings on the table.

60 Thirteen pence, a greyish handkerchief and two crumpled crisp packets.

'Thomas.'

A rubber **dimetrodon**, three pence and an oak leaf.

'Julie.'

'I haven't got pockets, Mr Doyle.'

65 Doyley smiled. 'Fair enough. Gerry.'

I took a deep breath, but to my surprise there was no stick of chalk amongst his belongings. His eyes met mine for a second.

'John T.'

John T. was John Turner from Class 11. There were so many Johns in
70 school that everyone was known by the first letter of their surname. Still no chalk. Just a marble, three paper clips and a creased Everton programme.

'John R.' I dug a hand into my pocket and gasped.

'Is there something wrong?' asked Doyley.

'No,' I said. 'I mean ...'

dimetrodon: *a large prehistoric reptile*

75 What *did* I mean? How could I
explain it? There, smooth and dangerous
at my fingertips was the incriminating
stick of chalk. Doyley said no more.
Instead he raised an enquiring eyebrow.

80 As I placed the chalk on his desk I
attempted an explanation. 'I don't know
how it got there, honest Mr Doyle.'

'The rest of you may get your lunch,'
said Doyley coolly. It was with dumb
85 helplessness that I watched the other
kids filing out. I suddenly understood
Neil's sly prod. As the door closed,
Doyley sat behind his desk.

'OK John,' he said, 'Let's hear what
90 you've got to say for yourself, son.'

MENU

Beefbangers make you burp

- BURGER ON A BUN.
- CURRY.
- CHIPS AND CURRY SAUCE.
- BAKED POTATO

Ganging Up *by Alan Gibbons*

Questions

1 Look again at lines 1–42. What do you learn about John's thoughts and feelings in these lines?

Help

In your answer you will need to write about:

a what John thinks about Gerry's behaviour
b how John reacts to Neil
c how Mrs McCartney makes John feel.

Remember

1 You will get better marks for this type of question if you can find details in the text to prove that your ideas are right. For every detail you mention in your answer you need to explain:

- what the detail shows
- how it shows it.

2 When you copy a word or phrase from the text make sure you:

- copy exactly
- put the word or phrase inside quotation marks.

3 If you are quoting more than three words, place your quotation on a new line.

4 If you have missed out part of a sentence in your quotation, show this by using an ellipsis (three dots). For example, 'Doyley … raised an enquiring eyebrow.' (lines 78–79)

2 Now look again at the section from line 42 to the end of the passage. The headmaster, Mr Doyle returns and is determined to find out who has written the graffiti on the board. How is the feeling of tension built up as Mr Doyle tries to find the guilty person?

Help

In your answer you need to write about:

a how the chalk is planted on John Ryan
b what John thinks and feels about what is happening
c how Mr Doyle investigates the situation
d the way in which the story is written.

Key points

1. The whole story is written just as if we are inside John's head, listening to his thoughts and aware of his feelings. To create this effect the writer uses 'I' to refer to John. When a story is told like this it is said to be using the **first person narrative**.

2. In a story told in first person narrative:
    a. You cannot get inside anyone else's head. This means that you never get to know what any of the other characters is thinking.
    b. You can only know as much as the narrator does, and then only what the narrator wants to tell you.
    c. In fact, you see the whole story from the narrator's **viewpoint**.

    One reason that tension builds up in this story is that you only get to see Gerry and Neil from John's point of view. Like John, you do not know that they can be so cunning, and since you are only aware of his thoughts and feelings you are expecting them to be caught and punished.

3. If you saw the story from Neil's point of view there would no sense of tension rising while Mr Doyle investigates, and then discovers, what has happened. You would have known for sure that he had planted the chalk on John. (Even if you did guess what had happened, you did not find out for certain until the end of the story.)

4. When there is trouble we side with our friends – the people we know best. In the same way, we sympathise with characters we know and like. It is John we feel sorry for when he realises how he has been tricked. In the book, the tension begins to mount again – will he find a way to get his own back?

Total exclusion zone

People have very different views on how to handle behaviour problems in schools. Read this article from *The Indy*, which discusses exclusion from school, then answer the questions on page 88.

Total exclusion zone

Expulsion or exclusion, whatever you call it, most teachers agree that when it happens, it's an admission of failure. But is there any alternative? **Arabella Warner** reports from schools around the country

TOBY TURNED up for his first day in his Barnsley secondary school in jeans and a jumper instead of his regulation school uniform. He was immediately suspended. His mother, who didn't believe in compulsory dress restrictions, advised him to keep going in, whereupon he was suspended a second time.

IT'S ROBSON. I GAVE HIM DETENTION IN 1978!

Then followed what can only be described as a charade – whenever Toby tried to get into school he found the way barricaded, or if he did manage to get in, he would be removed by the headmaster. Toby was also refused by the 18 other local schools. They claimed that although he himself did not constitute a threat, what he believed in did. Toby has been educated at home ever since.

Lorraine was 14 when she was eventually excluded from school in North London for stubbing out a cigarette on another girl's hand. This was the final episode in what had been a catalogue of violent behaviour, including beating up other girls. She now attends a special unit designed for children who cannot be taught in the regular school system.

Expulsion is a powerful weapon, but is it necessary? Mr Smith, headmaster of Bradfield Grammar School, believes it is. 'I don't do it very often – maybe once a year – for something which is a blatant defiance of the school rules, like a bad act of bullying or a major theft. But I never do it without a sense of failure.' Martin Penney, Chairman of the Society of Headmasters, is also a benign disciplinarian. 'I like to think that I have only ever expelled two pupils in my nine years as headmaster. They were for drug trafficking, which I abhor. If people can't cooperate with our very reasonable requests, then I think that it's best for everyone that they should go.'

Jane Wharton, co-ordinator for support services in Lambeth, runs units for children who don't fit into the school system – truants, pregnant teenagers and children who can't cope with school, as well as those who have been excluded from it. 'Permanent exclusion is a negative, but in some cases a necessary solution. Every school will have different thresholds of what they can tolerate, but if a teacher is consistently threatened and abused they are not going to wait until they are beaten up before they take any action. Once, a boy in my unit who I had regularly warned for his violent behaviour turned to me, threw every pot and pan he could lay his hands on at me, and then threatened me with a pair of kitchen scissors. I had no other choice but to exclude him, because I could no longer work with somebody who didn't understand that I was authority. It was an awful decision because after that he had nothing – his father was an alcoholic, his mother was in a wheelchair, and although he was now eligible for individual tuition, we have a waiting list of 60 people, for home tutors in Lambeth alone.'

I'M EXCLUDING YOU, BOY, FOR BEING ABLE TO AFFORD A MORE STYLISH HAIRCUT THAN MINE!

Jane does believe that in some cases exclusion is used badly. 'Some children are excluded for not wearing uniform or coming in late. Well, I would rather they did that than not come in at all. But teachers aren't sadistic, it's just that the pupil/teacher relationship breaks down. Other children just can't take the hugeness of the schools, and do better in a closer unit.' She quotes one example. 'We had a girl in who had been excluded from school for fighting. She kept phoning the Fire Brigade – until eventually I caught her at it. I put my hand on her shoulder to stop her, and she swung round and swore obscenely at me. Then when she had calmed down, she said, "You're lucky, I once knocked a teacher's teeth out for doing that." Because of her violent upbringing, she expected all relationships with adults to be violent, but the closeness of the unit had taught her to respect me.'

However, some people believe that children should never be excluded, and that there should always be a way of looking at each child's individual needs and integrating them in a class.

Temporary exclusion is seen by most people as useful for a period of cooling off, a breathing space in which school and family can come to some kind of agreement over how best to tackle a problem. But we don't live in an ideal world, and problems aren't always sorted out. Kelly was excluded from her East London school for three days when she was caught in a fight with a girl who had been consistently bullying her. When she returned to school the bullying not only got worse, but she was sent to Coventry by the bully's friends. In the end she decided the only solution was to go to another school.

Anne Wade from Education Otherwise, a support group for parents who decide to educate their children out of school, thinks that the answer lies in flexi-schooling, a system a bit like night school, since instead of forcing children to be at school, they attend because they actually want to.

But, in the education system as it stands, it does seem that exclusion and expulsion are necessary evils.

The Indy

Questions

1 Explain how each of the permanently excluded pupils in this report came to be excluded.

Help

Work through the first five paragraphs. Find out about:

a Toby

b Lorraine

c the two pupils Martin Penney excluded

d the boy that Jane Wharton had to exclude.

2 Give a brief account of the different attitudes shown to exclusions in this report. Make sure that you use **your own words** as far as possible.

Help

Make sure you cover:

a the headteachers in Barnsley (lines 1–18)

b Mr Smith of Bradfield Grammar (lines 28–35)

c Martin Penney (lines 35–42)

d Jane Wharton (lines 43–88)

e the people who do not believe in exclusion (lines 89–93)

f the views given on temporary exclusion (lines 94–108)

g Anne Wade (lines 109–115).

3 How do you think the writer tries to influence the reader on the subject of exclusions?

Help

Think about:

a the people selected for interview

b the effect of the section on Jane Wharton's work for pupils who do not fit into school

c the ways that the views of those who believe children should never be excluded are presented

d the conclusion of the report.

Key points

1   One of the questions here – question 2 – reminded you to write your answer in **your own words** as much as you can. Of course, you should do that with all your answers. There is not a lot of value in copying what someone else has written. When you are reminded to write in your own words, it is often because there is a question that could tempt you into copying.

2   Here you were asked to report on what people thought about exclusion. That meant doing two things:
    a   finding people's views in the report
    b   putting their thinking into **your** English.

As an example, look at how the headteachers in Barnsley responded to Toby, who refused to wear school uniform. Read lines 1–18 of the report again. The sentence which expresses the headteachers' view is not too difficult to find:

They claimed that although he himself did not constitute a threat, what he believed in did.

Even if the word 'constitute' is new to you, the general meaning can still be worked out: Toby was not the problem; what he was wearing was the problem.

3   So what can you say about the headteachers' views? At a first level, you can gain credit simply for recognising that, in Barnsley, headteachers are committed to exclusion if a pupil refuses to wear uniform.

4   At a higher level, you could gain more credit if you could explain the underlying problem. The headteachers claim it is what the family 'believes' that is the problem. Clearly they are not talking about religion here. The exclusion is to do with the fact that Toby's family thinks differently about what is right and wrong in school.

What The Teacher Said When Asked:
What Er We Avin For Geography Miss?

This morning I've got too much energy
much too much for geography

I'm in a high mood
so class don't think me crude
5   but you can stuff latitude and longitude

I've had enough of the earth's crust
today I want to touch the clouds

Today I want to sing out loud
and tear all maps to shreds

10   I'm not settling for river beds
I want the sky and nothing less

Today I couldn't care if east turns west
Today I've got so much energy
I could do press-ups on the desk
15   but that won't take much out of me

Today I'll dance on the globe
in a rainbow robe

while you class remain seated
on your natural zone
20   with your pens and things
watching my contours grow wings

All right class, see you later.
If the headmaster asks for me
say I'm a million dreaming degrees
25   beyond the equator

a million dreaming degrees
beyond the equator

by John Agard

Questions

1 The poem is supposed to be the teacher's answer to a question from a pupil asking what kind of lesson they are going to have.

What do we learn about the teacher's thoughts and feelings as she replies to the pupil's question?

 Help

In your answer you need to think about:
a the mood the teacher is in
b what the teacher wants to do
c what the teacher says about the subject she teaches
d how the teacher describes her pupils
e how the teacher's message to the headmaster at the end of the poem is written.

2 How does the poet make the poem lively and fun to read?

 Help

There is a lot more to write about for this answer. Start by trying to spot as many of these as you can:
a things that the teacher said which were surprising
b any humour you enjoyed
c all the contrasts the teacher uses (for example, between land and sky, east and west)
d the way words to do with geography are used
e any rhymes, rhythms and sound patterns – try to work out how these give the poem a sense of pace and energy
f any other details you enjoyed.

 Remember

You can only hear a rhythm or sound pattern, you cannot see one.

Listening to a poem is just as important as reading it on the page.

1 The way a poem is written should suit the ideas that are expressed in it. In this one, the teacher is not behaving in the way we would expect her to: she is saying she wants to be free from her responsibilities and just get out of here!

It is not surprising, then, that the poet uses words in unusual and extravagant ways for the teacher to express her ideas.

2 Really the teacher is saying that she wants to be the opposite of what she is now. For this reason it is rather fitting that she uses so many opposites to describe her mood – look at lines 6–7, 10–11, 12, and so on.

3 Even the way the poem is set out on the page adds to the idea that she wants to rebel. The poet has deliberately not used:
   - a regular rhyme scheme
   - regular stanzas
   - sentences (with one exception).

It is as if the poem is not in the mood for following rules, either.

4 The only time a sentence is used is in line 22. This is when the teacher has made her decision. She is not expressing a feeling any more, she is addressing her class. Her words are what you would expect from a teacher; they are an instruction – 'all right class, do this'. It seems fitting that these words are written more formally.

5 At the end of the poem the repetition suggests the teacher has escaped at last – if not in body, at least in her imagination. It just goes to show it is not only pupils who want to be set free from lessons!

B13 Waiting for the party

Cat normally lives with her grandmother (called the Pag) but she has just come to stay with her parents for a while. On the evening she arrives, her mother and father, who are both actors, are holding a party. They go off for a rest, leaving Cat all alone in an unfamiliar house.

I unpacked the duffel and put my clothes away and tried to read but I wasn't comfortable in my yellow room. It was like being shut up inside a daffodil. I opened the door and crept out, but when I got downstairs I didn't dare sit anywhere or touch anything. I would have liked to ring the Pag to say I had
5   arrived safely, but by the time I had found the telephone, hidden under a doll with silk skirts, the quiet in the house had really unnerved me; I was afraid of clearing my throat, let alone talking. I found the telly inside a polished cabinet with more glamorous portraits of my parents standing on top of it, but I couldn't turn it on in case it woke them up. I wanted a drink of water
10   and I found a glass in the clean, scrubbed, silent kitchen, but I was afraid it would make a terrible noise if I turned on the tap. In the Pag's house – *at home* – when you ran a bath or flushed the lavatory, the water thundered and crashed in the pipes as if there had been some enormous natural disaster, a tidal wave or a quake that might open the earth and swallow us up. The Pag
15   was always saying she must have it seen to, but she never did. She said there always seemed to be something more amusing to do than play about with the plumbing.

I went back to my yellow room.

I sat on the bed.

20   And waited.

I read a chapter of *Jane Eyre*.

And waited.

Then I changed into my black velvet mini skirt and white cashmere sweater.

25   And waited some more.

The house was dead quiet for *five hours*.

At the end of the longest afternoon of my life, there was *pandemonium*. Of course, they had slept too long! I should have woken them up! The party was due to start in just under an hour! They would never be ready in time!

30 They flew around the house, banging doors, swearing and yelling – at each other, at me. I couldn't see what the fuss was about. Reconnoitring in the kitchen during their **interminable** siesta I had noted the bottles of wine in the fridge and the plates of party nibbles covered with cling film. But my mother was gasping and sobbing and putting the back of her hand to her

35 forehead as if she was auditioning for a part in some exceptionally **harrowing** tragedy.

'I can't do it,' she moaned, 'I simply can't do it! I'm not even dressed!' Daddy-O had disappeared at this point so I was her only audience. I tried to think what the Pag would like me to do.

40 I said, 'I can put the food out. I can pour drinks. I can answer the door. There's nothing else to do, is there?'

She stopped her act instantly. 'Oh,' she said. '*Oh, duckie*, will you really? What a perfect *angel-pie* you are!'

She tripped merrily out of the kitchen and vanished upstairs. Daddy-O

45 appeared a few minutes later. He was wearing tight, purple trousers and a white shirt with big, billowing sleeves. This fancy gear made him look older. I thought – I couldn't be sure – that he was wearing lipstick.

He saw me looking at him. He said, 'Your mother likes to dress up.' He wasn't apologising. Just explaining.

50 I said, 'That's a beautiful shirt, Daddy-O.'

I thought, the Pag would be proud of me! I had meant to behave badly but it was turning out to be harder than I had expected. It would be like being beastly to a couple of kids.

interminable: *seeming to go on for ever*
harrowing: *upsetting*

She came down the stairs then, pausing at the bottom to twirl around so
55 that the skirt of her red dress flew out, showing her black lace tights right up
to her bottom.

Daddy-O caught her round the waist and danced her round the hall. I
stood at the kitchen door and watched them. Her hair had been sprayed so
hard it didn't move, and the false hair that covered his bald patch was stiff
60 and woolly.

Suddenly, I knew what they reminded me of. A pair of Barbie dolls! A
giggle burst out of me, I couldn't help it, but as the door chimes sang at that
moment I was able to turn it into a wildly excited laugh as I ran to the door.

Granny the Pag *by Nina Bawden*

Questions

In this unit you are only asked two questions about the passage, but you are
expected to explain your answer in a lot of detail. Use the help sections to
make sure you have selected the information you wish to write about.

1   Look closely at lines 1–17. What makes this house seem so
uncomfortable to Cat?

 Help

As you read through the description of Cat exploring the house, make
a note of:
  a   all the things Cat thinks of doing, and why she does not do them
  b   what Cat seems to dislike
  c   what seems to matter in this house compared to the Pag's house.

2   Now read lines 18–61 again. How does the author make you aware of
the excitement building up as the time for the party draws near?

 Help

Look closely at:
  a   how Cat passes the time when she is alone (lines 18–25).
        Think about the words that are repeated and the effect of
        the short sentences and paragraphs
  b   the sentences in lines 27–29
  c   what Cat's parents have already done to get the house ready for
        the party
  d   how Daddy-O and Cat's mother behave once they are awake
  e   how Cat feels by the time the doorbell rings.

Key points

An author builds a sense of mood or atmosphere through carefully chosen details.

Let us look now at how the author of *Granny the Pag* used:
- the **setting**
- the **feelings** and **behaviour** of her characters
- **description**

to build a sense of excitement while Cat waits for the party to begin.

1 The setting

The way the house has been prepared makes us wonder about the kind of party we can expect.

a Her parents 'glamorous photographs' are on display on the television. *Will other actors be coming? Who do they want to impress?*

b Her parents have made sure the house is immaculate: Cat does not dare touch anything. *Why does it have to be so clean and tidy?*

c The house is totally silent; it is unnerving. *Why do her parents need to rest for <u>five hours in absolute silence</u> before this party begins?*

2 Feelings and behaviour

We see how the excitement affects different characters.

a Cat feels nervous, so she creeps around the house not daring to touch or do anything. When she goes back to her room and waits and waits for her parents to wake up she becomes restless. She makes an effort to look nice for the party.

b When her parents do finally wake up there is a big change. Suddenly the house is filled with noise and activity as they rush about getting ready.

c Cat's mother is so excited she behaves more like a child than an adult. Her feelings change very quickly: one minute she is terribly worried and the next she is merrily calling Cat 'duckie' and 'angel-pie'.

3 Description

The author's descriptions of Cat's parents build up our expectations even more.

a Their reactions to waking up late – *they are so frantic that this party must be really special.*

b They dress up in an elaborate and theatrical way – *what kind of guests are they expecting? After all, Cat, who does not know their friends, is much more simply and plainly dressed.*

c They start dancing – *as if they cannot wait for the party to begin.*

B14 You can get a nice wash here!

Sipho and his friends are a group of black South African street children (*malunde*). One night they are seized and thrown into the back of a police van (a *gumba-gumba*) by a group of white men who are not wearing police uniforms.

Suddenly from outside the van there was a burst of laughter. A few seconds later the van doors were wrenched open. Sipho made out a hand being thrust in, then the sound of squirting. Even before the hand was pulled back and the door slammed shut, something was in their eyes, their nostrils, their mouths.

5 There was no air left to breathe, only something horribly foul stifling them. It smelt like the spray for killing insects. Coughing and trying to cover his mouth at the same time, Sipho felt he was going to be sick.

Now the *gumba-gumba* was moving, its engine revving and rumbling. Where were they being taken? It felt like they were travelling at speed, only

10 occasionally slowing down. Together they clustered at the far end of the van, holding on to each other, holding their stomachs tightly or trying to bury their faces and stinging eyes in their arms.

Suddenly the van gave an enormous shudder and Sipho found himself flung forward as it came to a bumping halt. He was the first to be grabbed as

15 the door swung open.

'OK, *vuilgoed*! Rubbish like you can get a nice wash here!'

Ahead of him, glinting through the darkness, Sipho saw water. He screamed as he was picked up. He tried to struggle once again but it was no use. The hands and arms were too powerful for him as they threw him out

20 into the lake.

Hitting, then breaking through the ice-cold water, his body shot out arms and legs in all directions. He couldn't swim. The more he fought with the water to get back up, the more he felt it was pulling him down. He was spluttering. The water was in his nose, in his mouth … He couldn't breathe.
25 He was sinking, his body pierced by a thousand freezing shocks.

Then a hand grasped his arm and he felt himself being slowly tugged until his foot touched something. Something solid which wasn't sinking beneath him. He brought his other foot down. He was standing! Stretching, he got his head enough above the water to gasp and gulp at the air. The hand led him
30 on a few more paces and then let go. A figure dived away from him. He was too confused to know who it was. Cries mingled with wild splashing sounds. On the bank ahead, he could just make out two large figures throwing a struggling shape out into the lake. Lucas? Laughter floated over to him. The *gumba-gumba* was revving up again. Within seconds the men had all climbed
35 inside and disappeared into the night.

Underneath his feet, Sipho felt things that were sharp. Painfully edging step by step, he forced himself forward through the water. His clothes, dripping and sticking to his body, felt unusually heavy. Shivering uncontrollably, he waded at last to the water's edge, pulled himself on to the
40 bank and flung himself down on his back. Directly above, as if staring down at him from the ink-black sky, was the moon, pale and white. Like a face. Was it laughing too?

One by one the other *malunde* joined him, shaking, swearing, sobbing.
Jabu was the last. His head bobbing in and out of the water, going down here
45 and coming up there, he guided those who were struggling towards the bank.
Such a strong swimmer … where did he learn it? thought Sipho. And weren't
his feet stinging too? Sipho pulled off his soaking canvas shoes. The thin soles
were torn and his feet were cut and bleeding. It was the same with the
others. People had thrown bottles into the lake which were lying at the
50 bottom, broken and sharp. Joseph and Matthew, however, emerged in an even
worse state. Finding bottles of *iglue* in their pockets, their attackers had
emptied them over their hair.

With water dripping from his clothes and trembling like the others,
Lucas insisted they leave immediately before any police arrived, but this time
55 in uniform.

'They can charge us for trespass!'

They could even be the same men who had thrown them into the lake, but
who would ever believe *malunde*?

No Turning Back by Beverley Naidoo

You can get a nice wash here!

Questions

1 In lines 1–35 the author describes how the group of boys are mistreated by the men. How is the increasing horror of what is happening built up?

? Help

Prepare to answer this question by looking at the effects of:

a the men's behaviour

b how Sipho and his friends react during the journey

c Sipho's thoughts and feelings when he is taken from the van and thrown into the lake

d the kind of Society the boys appear to live in.

2 Now look at lines 36–58. The men have gone, leaving the boys struggling in the water. Explain Sipho's thoughts and feelings about what has happened.

? Help

Prepare to answer this question by looking at:

a how Sipho feels as he gets out of the lake

b what the other boys have gone through

c why the boys must leave immediately.

Remember

When you are trying to work out the meaning of unfamiliar words:

• use the rest of the sentence and passage to help you work out what they must mean. Look at pages 39–41 for more help on how to do this.

If the whole text seems difficult:

• Read the text slowly and carefully.

• Work out one sentence at a time.

• Pause at the end of each sentence and try to understand what is going on.

• Try putting the main ideas into your own words before moving on to the next sentence.

• Read the text through several times.

• Focus on *what you can understand*:
  – get hold of the main ideas of the passage
  – use the main ideas to help you think about how the details work in the passage.

At first sight the world in which Sipho, Jabu, Lucas, Joseph and Matthew live may seem very different to the one you know. But is it?

When a story takes place in another time or another place, or is about groups of people who are unfamiliar to you, be prepared to work a bit harder to understand what is going on – you may find they are not so different after all.

1 Expect to meet unfamiliar words

When you meet words you do not know, see if you are told, or can work out, what they mean. In this story you should have been able to guess that *iglue* was probably some type of glue – you were told it was sticky, and the word looks similar to the English word.

Vuilgoed was harder, but, because of the way it is said and the rest of the speech you can tell it is an insult – which is all you need to know.

2 Look for clues in the text

As you read the text, look for clues about:
a what makes this society different from the one you are used to
b how people speak or behave towards each other.

This will help you to understand why characters have their particular problems, or behave the way they do.

3 Look out for familiar ideas

Make sure you spot the problems that characters are facing. Even if the details in a story are unfamiliar to you, the main ideas and the characters' problems are probably familiar.

You have just read about one group of characters bullying another group because of racial prejudice. We have the same problem in our society.

4 How are you expected to react?

Try to work out how you are expected to feel about the characters' problems. For example, the reader is expected to feel sorry for the black children in this passage because:

- you only see the events from their point of view
- all the black children are poor and defenceless
- all the white policemen are powerful and cruel.

B15

This tube ...

Look at the advertisement for the charity Sight Savers. Read it carefully, then answer the questions below.

Questions

1 What do you learn about trachoma in this advertisement?

 Help

Look at lines 1–16 and 25–58 of the advertisement. Think about

a what trachoma is

b what it does

c how it can be treated.

2 What do you discover about the charity Sight Savers?

 Help

Look at lines 17–24 and 25–58 of the advertisement. Think about:

a the name of the charity

b the age of the charity

c what it aims to do

d how it works.

3 How does this advertisement try to be effective as a fundraising appeal?

 Help

Look at the whole advertisement including:

- the headline and sub-headings
- the photographs.

Think about:

a words or phrases that suggest how serious the problem is

b word or phrases that show how simple the solution could be

c how the photographs reinforce the sense that a problem is being solved

d the prices that are mentioned

e the appeal of the last three paragraphs.

THIS TUBE WOULD SAVE THEIR SIGHT

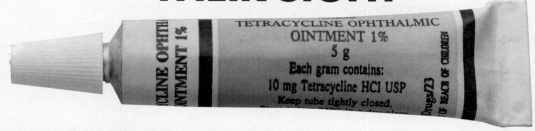

AND ALL IT COSTS IS £1.20

5.5 million people in the developing world are blind because of trachoma. 150 million more, three quarters of them children, are carrying the infection. 540 million people — 10% of the world's population — are at risk of developing the disease if it is not controlled.

Severe trachoma makes life impossible for young mothers trying to look after their children. Fathers struggle to work to support themselves and their families. Children cry themselves to sleep with the pain.

But the most horrifying thing is that all this suffering is totally unnecessary. Trachoma can be treated very quickly and cheaply in its early stages with a small tube of ointment called Tetracycline.

Delivery guaranteed

Sight Savers, or the Royal Commonwealth Society for the Blind as you may have known us previously, have been preventing and curing blindness in developing countries since 1950. We have over 40 mobile units that travel to remote villages and help identify those people suffering from trachoma.

It costs as little as £1.20 to treat one person

Someone suffering from trachoma could have their pain eased with a tube of soothing Tetracycline ointment. It only costs £1.20 to examine someone with trachoma and buy the ointment. But this is still too much for many people in the developing world.

That's why we're asking for your help. Childhood is the best time to attack the disease, before it takes hold. A gift of £12 would mean that ten young people would no longer have to suffer the torture of trachoma.

You can even help with more advanced cases. We can carry out an operation to turn back ingrown eyelashes on ten people suffering from trachoma with just £50.

And a Mobile Eye Unit that examines literally hundreds of people and also deals with many other blinding conditions costs just £125 to keep on the road for a week. Wouldn't you pay that without hesitation if it were your eyes at stake?

You've probably blinked a dozen times since you started reading this. If you were badly infected with trachoma, each of those blinks would be agony.

But in the blink of an eye you could send a gift and help release someone with trachoma from their suffering.

Please help. And thank you for sharing our vision of a world where no one needs to be unnecessarily blind.

Key points

1. Most questions asking you to respond to advertisements will ask something about their effect. Advertisements set out to sell you something. This does not mean they are all to be mistrusted. We need to know how to spend our money, and advertisements can contain useful information to help us make a choice. In the case of a charity, for example, you should not give unless you know what it will use the money for.

2. If you are asked to look at an advertisement, it is likely that the questions will cover two areas:
   a what the advertisement is telling you
   b how the advertisement tries to persuade you.

   Information and persuasion are not two separate issues. Fact and opinion are often closely linked. The advertisement tells us that operations on ten people with ingrown eyelashes cost £50. Clearly, most people will think that is good value. The advertisement presses the point by saying the cost is 'just £50'. The word 'just' adds an element of opinion to the fact of the cost. If we fail to react to the price itself, that single word encourages us to think of £50 as good value.

3. When you are looking at the effect of an advertisement, remember these things.

   • The heading and any sub-headings are an important part of the whole message – people tend to see these before they read the detail.

   • The pictures/photographs are a powerful part of the whole image that is being presented.

   • You must make it clear why you think a word or a phrase works well. If you choose to comment on the word 'guaranteed', you need to say more than 'it is effective'. You could say that it helps to suggest that here is a charity that keeps its promises. You could say that the charity is trying to sell itself and wants to imply that it carries a guarantee in the same way as other high-quality goods. The reason you give is up to you, but it must be given and it must make sense to the reader.

B16 The night the men came

Marga Minco's book *Bitter Herbs* tells the story of her childhood in Holland and how it was affected by the Nazi occupation of that country. The following extract recounts the last moments before her parents are taken prisoner. Marga was the only member of her family who escaped death in a concentration camp.

As you read, think about the way the passage contrasts details of ordinary family life with an awareness of an ever-present threat.

The night the men came I ran away, through the back garden door.

It had been a mild spring day. In the afternoon we had lain in deckchairs in the garden, and in the evening I noticed that my face was already slightly sunburnt.

5   Mother had been ill the whole week, but she had been well enough again to lie out in the sun that afternoon. 'Tomorrow I'm going to start knitting a summer jumper for you,' she promised me. Father lay smoking a cigar in silence, and left his book unopened on his lap. In the tool shed I had found a tennis racket and a ball, with which I practised a bit, against the wall. The
10 ball constantly flew over the top, and then I had to open the garden door and go and look for it in the road. And sometimes it landed on the other side of the fence. Between our garden and the neighbours' was a narrow ditch, with a board fence on either side of it. You could just stand upright in the narrow passage without being seen.

15 While I was searching for my ball there, Father came to have a look.

'That'd make a nice hiding-place,' he said.

He climbed over the fence and we squatted behind a tree which belonged neither to us nor to the neighbours. Our feet sunk into the soft earth, and it smelt of rotten leaves there. While we sat thus hidden in the dimness,
20 Father whistled.

'Hullo,' he called.

'Where have you two got to?' asked my Mother. She seemed to have been dozing.

'Can you see us?' Father asked.

25   'No. Where *are* you?'

'Here,' Father said, 'on the other side of the fence. Just use your eyes.'

We peered through a crack and saw Mother drawing nearer.

'I still can't see you,' she said.

'Just the job,' said Father. He straightened up and sprang agilely over the
30 fence. 'Stay sitting where you are for a minute,' he said to me. He intimated
to my Mother that it was her turn to try to climb over the fence.

'But why?'

'Just try,' he replied.

Mother had to repeat the performance several times before she did it
35 nimbly enough to please my Father. Then he climbed back over the fence
himself, and all three of us squatted down together in the ditch.

'No one will ever think of looking for us here,' he said. 'Let's stay here for a
bit, to see whether we can stick it out for long in this position.'

But I espied my ball among the leaves. 'I'm going to practise backhand,'
40 I cried, and jumped back into the garden. My Father and Mother remained
sitting where they were.

'Can you see us?' Father called.

'No,' I called back. 'I can't see anything.'

They reappeared. My Mother dusted herself down. 'I've got absolutely
45 filthy in that place,' she said.

'To-morrow I'll dig out a hole, and rake the leaves away a bit, so that we
can sit there in more comfort,' my Father promised.

That evening, after dinner, I stood in front of the window, looking out. The
street was deserted. It was so quiet that you could hear the birds chirping.

50   'Do come away from that window,' said Mother.

'Where's the harm in it? There's not a soul in sight,' I said. Nevertheless I
turned and sat down. My Mother poured out the tea. Softly she moved about
between the tea trolley and us.

'Perhaps it would be better if we didn't take any tea,' said my Father.
55 'Then we can make a quicker getaway to the garden if they should come.'

'It's so *cheerless* here without tea,' my Mother objected.

Slowly the darkness came down. As Father was pulling the curtains shut
the first truck roared past.

He stood still, holding the curtain in his hand, and looked at us.

60   'There they go,' he said.

'They're going by,' said Mother. We listened to those sounds from outside. The roar of the trucks' engines died away. The silence lasted for some time. Then we heard more heavy vehicles pass along the street. This time it took longer for the noise to cease. But then a silence fell which we hardly dared to
65 break. I saw my Mother looking at her half-full teacup, and I knew she wanted to finish drinking her tea. But she did not move.

After a while my father said: 'We'll wait another ten minutes and then we'll put the big light on.' But before those ten minutes were up the bell rang.

It was just before nine. We remained sitting where we were, and looked at
70 each other in surprise. As if we were asking ourselves: who could that be? As if we didn't know! As if we thought: it's just as likely to be a friend or acquaintance, dropping in for a visit! After all, it was still early in the evening, and tea had been made.

They must have had a master key.

75 They were standing in the room before we could stir. Two tall men, wearing light raincoats.

Bitter Herbs by Marga Minco

Questions

1 How does this passage give an impression of ordinary life continuing under Nazi occupation?

 Help

Look at lines 2–14. Think about:
a the kind of day it was
b what people were doing
c the impression that these details create.

Look at lines 44–56. Think about the mother's reaction:
a about her clothes
b about taking tea
c about the impression created by her concern for these things.

2 How does the writer build up a sense that something which will threaten family life is about to happen?

 Help

Think about:
a the opening paragraph
b the 'game' of hiding between the fences
c the look of the street after dinner
d the concern about the window
e the worry about the tea
f the effect of the trucks
g the way the men appear.

 Remember

When you choose words from the passage you need to explain **why** you have chosen them.

Key points

1 When you read, there needs to be something to encourage you to keep reading. In the case of stories, the thing that most often keeps you turning the page is the desire to find out what happens next.

 In this story, the writer chooses to let you know at the very start of the chapter that the 'men' are going to come. You read on to discover who the men are and what happens when they arrive. Perhaps it will not be as serious as it sounds, perhaps it will be even worse. Only by reading on can you be sure.

2 This extract covers one of those situations where the reader knows more than the characters in the story. The little details of ordinary life leave you wanting to say 'That's not going to last' just as you used to yell 'He's behind you!' at the pantomime.

 In spite of the fact that you cannot warn them, the family are clearly aware of the danger, and much of the father's thinking is focused on escape and hiding. Perhaps that is why he never settles to reading his book in the afternoon sunshine.

3 The details of ordinary family life and the nearness of the Nazi threat provide a key contrast in this extract. **Contrast** is important to many kinds of writing and is crucial here. It is essential to understand about contrasts because you will come across them on many occasions.

4 Sometimes you may be asked two separate questions about the contrasting sides of a piece of writing, as in this unit. At other times, you may be given a single question in which you are asked to make the contrast yourself.

5 If you are asked to write about a contrast in one main question, you must organise yourself in much the same way as for the two questions here. You need to:

 a search out the detail for both sides of the contrast

 b be clear about what the contrast does.

 Here, the ordinary little details of life help to make the possible destruction of the family's world seem that little bit more monstrous.

In the poem below, the poet is describing how two woodmen, Job and Ike, throw a very old tree. 'Throwing' was a word used in the nineteenth century for chopping down a tree. Although the poet admires their skill, he has mixed feelings about what they are doing.

Throwing a Tree

The two executioners stalk along over the knolls,
Bearing two axes with heavy heads shining and wide,
And a long limp two-handled saw toothed for cutting great boles,
And so they approach the proud tree that bears the death-mark on its side.

5   Jackets doffed they swing axes and chop away just above ground,
And the chips fly about and lie on the moss and fallen leaves;
Till a broad deep gash in the bark is hewn all the way round,
And one of them tries to hook upward a rope, which at last he achieves.

The saw then begins, till the top of the tall giant shivers;
10   The shivers are seen to grow greater each cut than before;
They edge out the saw, tug the rope; but the tree only quivers,
And kneeling and sawing again, they step back to try pulling once more.

Then, lastly, the living mast sways, further sways: with a shout
Job and Ike rush aside. Reached the end of its long staying powers
15   The tree crashes downward: it shakes all its neighbours throughout,
And two hundred years' steady growth has been ended in less than two hours.

by Thomas Hardy

Remember

Even when you are tackling an older poem you need to remember that the **way it is written** is just as important as what it means.

Questions

1 How does the poet make the tree seem so impressive?

? Help

In your answer you should include:
a what we know about the tree
b how the tree is described
c how the death of the tree is described
d the way the poem is written.

2 Explain the poet's thoughts and feelings about the men and their work.

? Help

In your answer you should include:
a the way the poet describes the workmen in the first stanza
b what he tells you about the way they work
c the last two lines of the poem
d anything else you think is important.

Remember

You may want to use the same quotation in both answers. If so, make sure that in each case you show that the quotation does actually help to answer the question.

🔑 Key points

Poems written a long time ago may use unfamiliar language, and the poet's ideas may seem strange to you. Even so, although you may have to work a little harder, it is possible to understand what is going on and to appreciate how the poet chose to write.

1   Start working on an older poem by thinking about **what** the poem is doing.
    a   Is it telling a story?
    b   Is it describing someone or something?
    c   Is it exploring an idea, or an emotion – such as love or anger?

    The poem in this unit tells the story of how an old and magnificent tree is chopped down by two men. Through it the poet is looking, with sadness, at how easily humans can destroy nature.

2   Once you are happy that you have grasped what the poem is about, you can look at **how** the ideas are expressed.

    The poet calls the woodcutters 'executioners', and we do not find out it is a tree they are going to kill until the third line. From the start this makes it clear how the poet feels.

3   Look for **details and images** which strike you as interesting. Then work out how they fit in with the main idea of the poem.

    You could choose a phrase like 'the tall giant shivers' from line 9. Calling the tree a giant makes it seem almost human, which increases our sympathy for it. Shivering is something we do when we are afraid, so it makes us think that the tree is afraid.

4   Make sure you read the poem aloud or in your head several times, and listen for its **sounds.**
    a   In earlier times poets were much more likely to use regular patterns of rhythm or rhyme and then change them for effect.
    b   The sounds of the words and phrases may also be important.

    If you notice something: **STOP**. Think about *how* the detail you have spotted adds to the poem.

5   A poem about a happy theme might have a bouncy rhythm and a quick **pace**. This one, which is about sadder things, is much slower and has heavier sounding words. Not surprisingly it also has long lines. This all slows the pace down. In fact the poem sounds like the sort of commentary you hear on sad state occasions. All this makes the death of the tree a solemn and important event.

6   Finally, remember that **if a detail is included, it is there because it matters**. This is as true of older poems as it is of modern ones.

B18 Run for your life

This is a longer passage for you to tackle. As you read it through, make sure you keep track of what is happening to Arnold, and how he thinks and feels about what is happening to him.

Arnold is in danger. He thought he would be safe if he hid in an old manor-house, especially if he kept out of sight by lying under a blanket. But Arnold was wrong. Boris, his enemy, has realised where Arnold is, and sent one of his men to deal with him.

Arnold lay back, clammy with fright. He could hear his heart hammering, as if it was in his head, not his chest. Of course, Boris knew he was in the ballroom and he had told his murdering minders …

5 He lay still, holding his breath to try and catch the smallest sound. His first panic had been overtaken by a rather familiar determination in the face of danger. He would have to rely on his wits now, if this was a man intending to kill him.

The ancient wooden floor sighed to the footsteps passing. A faint creak … there was no doubt someone was in the room. A ray of torchlight flickered 10 momentarily on a row of white skulls and faded. Now Arnold could hear the footsteps approaching. He held his breath. If the torch came looking under the staging, he would be lost.

He pulled the blanket right over him and held up a corner to see through. In the dim light – his eyes becoming accustomed – he saw a pair of legs 15 walking past, very slowly. The torchlight was searching the stacked chairs, screens and various rubbish that lined the far wall. Arnold could see no higher than the man's behind.

Opposite Arnold was the small Exit door that let out at the back of the hall. He knew it was unlocked. If the intruder did not give up but came 20 searching more thoroughly, Arnold decided to make a bolt for it. He stood far more chance out in the open, could run like a hare if his life depended on it. The legs disappeared out of vision, returning to the front of the orchestra stand. Arnold dithered as to whether to go or not. But betted on the intruder departing, having found nothing. Wrongly, as it turned out.

25 The man went up to the top of the hall again and there was a long and wracking silence. Then the footsteps came again over the creaking floor, round the back of the staging. This time the torch was turned inward.

Arnold ran. The man was still out of his vision, round the curve of the staging, and Arnold, doubled up, went silently, hoping to get to the door
30 unseen. But as he straightened up to open the door, a board creaked beneath his foot. The torch flew in his direction, pinning him in its bright light.

He wrenched at the door handle and flung himself through the door. The man came after him. Instead of running straight, Arnold right-angled and ran down the back wall to the corner, then launched off among the pine trees
35 in the direction of the river.

The torchlight caught him, lost him as he leapt sideways and fell in landing. The uneven ground had dropped him into a nice hole. Taking advantage, he turned and crawled and wriggled back in the opposite direction, keeping his head down, following an animal track. The man ran
40 to the spot where the light had picked him out and stood there, flashing the torch all round. Arnold froze to the ground.

His pursuer was about five metres away. Arnold buried his face into the earth and waited. The torchlight flickered all round like a will-o'-the wisp over the dank heather.
45 Arnold could hear the man's heavy, angry breathing and the squelching of his feet as he moved direction. The man knew he was there and persisted, searching, but when he decided to stamp his way around the area to flush
50 Arnold out, he fortunately chose the down-river direction, and turned his back for a few moments.

Arnold took the opportunity to wriggle a little further. It was imperative to make no noise. Fortunately the river rolling over loose rocks made a
55 grumbling, gravelling noise which covered up the rustling of his snakelike progress. He put several more metres between himself and the searcher before the torch turned back uphill in his direction.

He lay still again, face down. It was only chance that would see him through. The man stamped backwards and forwards, at one point coming to
60 within an arm's length. His stamping foot flicked wet earth in Arnold's face. Arnold stopped breathing; his pulse thumped so loud it seemed to fill the night. But his luck held. Within centimetres of him, the man swore and muttered and turned away. The torchlight went on down to the river and Arnold heard cursing and crashings, but gradually the sound of pursuit receded.

65   Arnold crawled on along a sketchy tunnel made by animals, making uphill for the track which he knew led away from the big house up the valley. He thought, if he made back to the house, the man would be lying in wait for him and in the other direction lay safety. If he lifted his head he could see the lights of the old fortified manor-house
70 some eight hundred metres away, looking very inviting, safe and cosy. But it would be suicide to go back. He had no alternative.

He laid up for about half an hour, cold, wet, and shivering. A half moon came out from behind the clouds and lit up the silent valley and let loose a few
75 glittering stars to wink at him from above the fell tops. Nothing moved.

Very carefully Arnold crept to his feet and, hunching down, started to move up the valley. All was quiet. Gradually he straightened up, moving
80 fast, but there was no pursuit. He had no idea what lay up the valley but it must be better than what lay in wait in the other direction.

The Boy Who Wasn't There *by K. M. Peyton*

Remember

When you are tackling a longer passage, split it up into smaller sections. Take each smaller section in turn and look at it closely.

Use the ideas in Unit A8 starting on page 39, to help you deal with any difficult words.

Questions

1 Arnold is trying to get away from the man. Look at lines 1–64. How does the writer build up and keep a feeling of danger in this part of the passage?

Help

In your answer you should comment on:
  a   Arnold's feelings, thoughts and hopes
  b   what Arnold can hear and see
  c   what Arnold does
  d   how the man who is searching for him reacts.

You should also think about how the passage is written:
  a   how the writer uses long and short sentences to speed up or slow down the pace as you read the text.
  b   how the writer describes the man chasing Arnold
  c   the way the torch and its movements are described.

2 Look at lines 65–82 again. Explain what Arnold's thoughts and feelings are, now that the man has gone.

Help

You will find this question easier to answer if you think about:
  a   Arnold's thoughts and feelings as time passes
  b   the plans he makes
  c   Arnold's thoughts about the manor house.

Key points

1   When you are asked a question about how the passage is written you need to look closely at the language. It helps if you focus on small parts of the text.

2   To start with, choose a place where the author is describing something. For example, the two short sentences below describe Arnold's fear.

Arnold lay back, clammy with fright. He could hear his heart hammering, as if it was in his head, not his chest.

Look carefully at the words used and ask yourself:
- Is there a striking image?
- Is there a particularly powerful verb?
- Is there a descriptive word?

In the passage the word 'clammy' makes us realise that Arnold has been sweating – this explains why he is damp, but it also tells us that he is feeling cold.

The verb 'hammering' tells us that Arnold's heart is beating so furiously that it is pounding away like a machine. In the second sentence the writer tells us that his heartbeat sounds so loud to Arnold that he almost thinks it is sounding in his head. We realise then just how powerful the fear must be if it makes his heart resound all the way through his body.

3   Once you have thought about individual words and phrases, then look at sentences and paragraphs.
- Short, simple sentences read more quickly and increase the pace of a piece.
- Longer, more complex sentences make for slower reading and a slower pace.

If you notice that a writer has used a lot of long or short sentences or paragraphs together, think about why this part of the text may need to be told at a slower or faster pace.

The sentences we looked at earlier are short, so they increase the pace. This suits the fact that this is an exciting moment in the story: Arnold is scared that the man will capture him.

B19 Rock bottom

Read the magazine article, then answer the questions on page 120.

rock bottom

Alcatraz, a rocky island in the San Francisco Bay, once housed the world's most notorious criminals. Although the prison has been closed for more than 30 years, it is a very popular tourist attraction. York Membery reports.

A rocky little island, shrouded in fog, looms ahead. A watchtower stands ominously over the fortress-like structure. As you approach, you see that the entire complex is surrounded by 15ft high concrete walls and barbed wire.

This was the chilling sight that greeted the first batch of inmates who arrived at Alcatraz in 1934, ready to be confined to the world's most notorious prison.

The 53 prisoners had been loaded onto a train more than 1,000 miles away. So deadly was the human cargo — which included America's public enemy Number One, Al Capone — that every man was clamped in leg-irons and chained to his seat; the train was fitted with barred windows and wire mesh doors.

All of them were being locked away in this hell-hole jail, from which there was no escape, for one reason: they were too dangerous ever to be allowed to walk the streets again.

Today the bad guys have gone and this island in San Francisco Bay has been turned into a tourist attraction. A million visitors a year are now drawn by the legends of Capone and wonderfully named gangsters like George 'Machine Gun' Kelly, Basil 'The Owl' Banghart and 'Creepy' Karpis, as well as Robert Stroud, the famous Birdman of Alcatraz (who spent 54 years of his life in prison, 44 of them in **solitary confinement**).

But even today, the very name Alcatraz sends a shiver down people's spines. The 12-acre island was christened La Isla de las Alcatraces (Island of the Pelicans), more than 200 years ago when California was under Spanish rule, but renamed Fort Alcatraz when the US Army took control in the 1800s. It became a civilian prison in 1934.

New inmates would be strip-searched on arrival and then put in **quarantine** for a

solitary confinement: *being locked up on your own*
quarantine: *a time of isolation away from other prisoners*

month. Then a mind-numbingly dull daily routine began that could last years, if not decades. Woken at 6.30am, they would
55 be marched in single file to the kitchen for breakfast. They had 20 minutes to eat their meal before being taken to a workshop, where the jobs included making uniforms and operating the
60 laundry. Prisoners would work solidly until 4.30pm, with the exception of a 20-minute lunch-break, and be back in their cells by 5.30pm. Lights out was at 9.30pm.

Kept in solitary confinement, the men
65 were not allowed to eat together, read newspapers, listen to the radio or even talk. However, there was a library — though books containing violence and crime were banned!

70 'If an inmate couldn't read he was in a whole lot of trouble because that was all he could do in the evening,' recalls ex-guard Frank Heaney. 'That's when they start flipping out'.

75 And flipping out was the one thing you didn't want to do on Alcatraz. For that was sure to earn a prisoner a spell on dreaded D-Block — or Dog Block — where inmates were locked up 24 hours a day,
80 seven days a week, surviving on a diet of bread and water, leaving the cells only for a ten-minute shower once a week. One man spent a staggering 97 days under this regime.

85 'The cells had a 200lb steel door so that when you close it you're in complete darkness day and night,' says Heaney. 'We'd give them a mattress at night-time but take it away during the day'. If that
90 didn't work, an inmate would be thrown naked into The Kennel, a cold, damp cell with just a hole in the floor. It's hardly surprising that prisoners spent their lives dreaming up ever more fantastic ways to
95 escape 'Hellcatraz'. At least 39 made a bid for freedom. But if the guards didn't get you (seven inmates were shot to death and 26 captured), the icy waters (one drowned) or the strong currents
100 more than likely would. The five missing men are believed to have been swept out to sea. But, who knows, maybe they're still around.

Questions

1 What does this article tell us about Alcatraz and its history?

 Help

Use the following questions to help you build up the information you need. You can write this information in note form but remember, you are going to use it so it has to be readable!

a Where is Alcatraz?
b What is it used for now?
c What has it been used for over the years?
d What was special about it as a place?
e How big is it?
f What did the Spaniards call it?
g Who took it over from the Spaniards and when?

2 What were prison routines like on Alcatraz?

 Help

Think about:
a what happened when they arrived
b the daily routine
c work
d leisure

3 How does the language used in the article build up a sense of the horror of prisons, especially Alcatraz?

 Help

When you choose words or phrases from the article, explain how they add to the impression of horror.

Key points

1   When you are answering questions, a key skill is knowing what to leave out. Many people get tempted into writing everything down without bothering to stop and think whether it is relevant or not. The mark schemes that examiners use often take away marks if you add in material that you do not need in your answer.

    There is nothing worse than doing the work to gain marks only to lose them as you write on and on!

2   The second question, for example, asked you to describe the prison routines at Alcatraz. The last part of the article dealt with escapes. Although the escapes involved prisoners, they are not actually a part of regular life of the prison so they are not relevant to the second question. The temptation to add it in is increased if you are interested in the escapes!

3   The other point about selecting material is the level of detail that you provide in your answer. For example, the first question here asked you about Alcatraz and its history.

    • Clearly you need to say that it was used as a prison.

    • It seems quite reasonable to add that it was a high-security prison, and perhaps that it was used for the most dangerous prisoners.

    • If you then begin to add all the names of the prisoners, you are almost beginning to repeat the whole article.

      If you escape losing marks for this, you are certainly losing time and risk not being able to finish your work.

B20 Getting up

It is early morning and time for Caithleen to get up. Through her eyes we learn what life used to be like for a young Catholic girl growing up in Ireland. Downstairs a workman called Hickey is already busy in the kitchen cooking her breakfast.

I rested for a moment on the edge of the bed, smoothing the green satin bedspread with my hand. We had forgotten to fold it the previous night, Mama and me. Slowly I slid on to the floor and the linoleum was cold on the soles of my feet. My toes curled up instinctively. I owned slippers but Mama
5 made me save them for when I was visiting aunts and cousins; and we had rugs but they were rolled up and kept in drawers until visitors came in the summer-time from Dublin.

I put on my ankle socks.

There was a smell of frying bacon from the kitchen, but it didn't cheer me.

10 Then I went over to let up the blind. It shot up suddenly and the cord got twisted round it. It was lucky that Mama had gone downstairs, as she was always lecturing me on how to let up blinds properly, gently.

The sun was not yet up, and the lawn was speckled with daisies that were fast asleep. There was dew everywhere. The grass below my window, the
15 hedge around it, the rusty paling wire beyond that and the big outer field were each touched with a delicate, wandering mist. And the leaves and the trees were bathed in the mist, and the trees looked unreal, like trees in a dream. Around the forget-me-nots that sprouted out of the side of the hedge were haloes of water. Water that glistened like silver. It was quiet, it was
20 perfectly still. There was smoke rising from the blue mountain in the distance. It would be a hot day.

Seeing me at the window, Bull's-Eye came out from under the hedge, shook himself free of water, and looked up lazily, sadly, at me. He was our sheep-dog and I named him Bull's-Eye because his eyes were speckled black and white, like canned sweets. He usually slept in the turf-house, but last night he had stayed there to be on the watch-out when Dadda was away. I need not ask, my father had not come home.

25

Just then Hickey called from downstairs. I was lifting my nightdress over my head, so I couldn't hear him at first.

'What? What are you saying?' I asked, coming out on to the landing with the satin bedspread draped around me.

30

'Good God, I'm hoarse from saying it.' He beamed up at me, and asked, 'Do you want a white or a brown egg for your breakfast?'

'Ask me nicely, Hickey, and call me dotey.'

'Dotey. Ducky. Darling. Honeybunch, do you want a white or a brown egg for your breakfast?'

35

'A brown one, Hickey.'

'I have a gorgeous little pullet's egg here for you,' he said as he went back to the kitchen. He banged the door. Mama could never train him to close doors gently. He was our workman and I loved him. To prove it, I said so aloud to the Blessed Virgin who was looking at me icily from a gilt frame.

40

'I love Hickey,' I said. She said nothing. It surprised me that she didn't talk more often. Once she had spoken to me and what she said was very private. It happened when I got out of bed in the middle of the night to say an **aspiration**. I got out of bed six or seven times every night as an act of **penance**. I was afraid of hell.

45

'Yes, I love Hickey,' I thought; but of course what I really meant was that I was fond of him. When I was seven or eight I used to say I would marry him. I told everyone, including the **catechism examiner**, that we were going to live in the chicken-run and that we would get free eggs, free milk, and vegetables from Mama. Cabbage was the only vegetable they planted. But now I talked less of marriage. For one thing he never washed himself, except to splash rainwater when he stooped-in over the barrel in the evenings. His teeth were green, and last thing at night he did his water in a peach-tin that

50

aspiration: prayer
penance: an action Caithleen does as part of her religion to show she is sorry for the bad things she does
catechism examiner: the person who tests Caithleen's understanding of her religion by asking her questions

55 he kept under his bed. Mama scolded him. She used to lie awake at night
waiting for him to come home, waiting to hear him raise the window while he
emptied the peach-tin contents on to the **flag** outside.

'He'll kill those shrubs under that window, sure as God,' she used to say,
and some nights when she was very angry she came downstairs in her
60 nightdress and knocked on his door and asked him why he didn't do that sort
of thing outside. But Hickey never answered her, he was too cunning.

I dressed quickly, and when I bent down to get my shoes I saw fluff and
dust and loose feathers under the bed. I was too miserable to mop the room,
so I pulled the covers up on my bed and came out quickly.

65 The landing was dark as usual. An ugly stained-glass window gave it a
mournful look as if someone had just died in the house.

'This egg will be like a bullet,' Hickey called.

'I'm coming,' I said.

The Country Girls by Edna O'Brien

flag: stone pavement

Questions

1 How does the writer make Caithleen's early home life seem attractive?

 Help

You should consider:
  a the way the garden is described
  b how Hickey treats Caithleen
  c the way in which humour is used
  d the writer's choice of detail and language.

You will find it helpful to read the Key points on the opposite page,
before you begin to plan your answer.

2 Look closely at lines 30–68. How does the writer make us aware that
Caithleen is growing up?

 Help

You should consider:
  a the way Caithleen treats Hickey
  b the things she understands about both Hickey and her mother
  c how her thoughts and feelings towards Hickey have changed
  d the words she uses to express her thoughts.

Key points

1 When you are asked to look at very detailed descriptive writing in a passage where there is not much action, it is important to break the text up into manageable sections. If you then look carefully at each one in turn you should find you have plenty to write about.

2 The passage you have just read could be split into several descriptions:
   - the country scene outside Caithleen's window
   - the room in which she wakes
   - the workman, Hickey
   - her thoughts and feelings as she gets up.

3 When you look at a particular description you may find that the author has chosen words or phrases which are linked in some way. The description of the view across the lawn contains many words to do with water. It describes the dampness as 'delicate wandering mist', and says it 'bathed' the leaves and trees. There are 'haloes of water', and 'water that glistened like silver'.

4 Each of these watery images is positive. A halo is a symbol of goodness, silver is a precious metal, the mist is 'delicate' and 'wandering' making it sound light and pretty – even lively. By putting several images of beauty together, the writer builds a whole scene which is attractive.

5 As you listen to the words used in these lines notice also how there are lots of light delicate sounds and long, winding sentences which make it seem slow and gentle. It is a pleasure to read. You may be used to listening to the sound of words in poetry, but in very descriptive prose they can be just as important.

B21 Snake curry

Maria Coffey and her husband Dag are exploring Vietnam. Their guide, Binh, has brought them to a restaurant owned by a man called Chin.

Quickly, we clambered up the steep bank and into a restaurant that overlooked the river. On a counter top by the doorway was a demi-john filled with a clear liquid and several fat snakes curled up like lengths of rope.

'First we drink the snake wine,' announced Binh casually. 'Then we eat the
5   snake.'

The owner of the restaurant appeared from the kitchen. He wore only a pair of loose cotton shorts and a grimy towel around his neck. He filled four small glasses from the demi-john and brought them over to us, staggering a little and grinning broadly to display his one and only fang-like tooth. While
10   we sipped the snake wine, which tasted like home brewed vodka, he explained the origin of his name, which was *Chin*, or nine. He was the youngest of eight children. As was traditional in Vietnam, his parents had named his eldest sibling *Hai*, or Two, to fool the evil spirits that are said to snatch away first-born children. Then the second born in his family was
15   named *Ba*, or Three, the third born *Bon*, Four, and so on until they got to *Chin*. The telling of this involved another round of snake wine. By now my head was beginning to spin.

'I have to eat soon,' I told Binh.

'Chin want to know which snake you like to eat,' he said.

20   'Cobra's her favourite,' joked Dag.

This was duly conveyed to Chin, who disappeared into the kitchen. Minutes later he was back. Instead of a towel around his neck he had a snake. About three feet long, it had a brown back and a cream and black striped belly. Chin placed it on the table, holding onto its tail. It slithered
25 across the Formica towards me, its tongue flickering in and out.

'He say it no poisonous,' said Binh, who had pushed his chair to a safe distance away from the table.

Chin picked up the writhing snake and placed it on Dag's knees.

'For God's sake, don't let it go up your shorts!' I cried.

30 Coolly, Dag picked it up by the base of its head.

'He say price of snake is 35,000 dong,' called Binh, who was now halfway across the room. 'He cook it with the vegetable and spice and hot chilli.'

'Good deal,' said Dag, carefully examining the snake. 'We'll take it.'

While Dag and Binh had another glass of wine, I followed Chin and the
35 snake into the kitchen. It was a gloomy room with only one small window. Two other men were in there, chopping vegetables on a stone counter, while Chin's wife squatted next to a large wok of water heating up over a charcoal burner.

'Hi hi!' shouted the men when they saw me. 'How old you? You have **babysan**?'

40 Perhaps sensing what was to come, the snake had wrapped itself tightly around Chin's arm. After carefully unravelling it, he dropped it into the steaming water. The snake didn't take too kindly to this; arching its back, it threw itself out of the wok and began wriggling towards a dark corner. The two men leapt about, whooping loudly, Chin's wife screamed and ducked
45 behind me, while Chin lunged after the snake.

Grabbing it by the tail, he flipped it back into the water, which was now vigorously boiling, and held it there with the end of a wooden spoon while it writhed around in what looked like agonizing death throes.

> **You have babysan?:** *the men want to know if Maria is already married.*

'How long does it take a snake to die?' I asked Dag, who had heard the
50 commotion and come running into the kitchen.

'It's already dead, those movements are just reflexes,' he said, in his best
veterinarian's voice.

At last the snake was still, its jaws wide open as if it had expired screaming.

'I've always liked snakes,' said Dag, ten minutes later.

55 This was just as well, because he was about to eat one. The creature had
been chopped into chunks, fried, and doused in a thick sauce.

'You try, very delicious,' said Binh, who had pulled his chair back to the table.

I used the end of my chop sticks to investigate the sauce which had a
strong curry flavour. Dag was using his to pick up a piece of snake.

60 'I'm forever amazed by what you'll put in there,' I commented, as the
chunk of flesh disappeared into his mouth.

Half a minute later, some rather surprising things came out. First a
sizeable piece of bone, then some skin that he'd sucked clean of sauce to
reveal cream and black markings and some nicely defined scales. Catching
65 Chin's eye, I ordered an omelette.

Three Moons in Vietnam by Maria Coffey

veterinarian: *Dag is trying to sound*
knowledgeable, like a vet

Remember

When you re-read the passage, you are looking for words and
phrases to help you support your answers.

Questions

1 **What impression of Dag do you gain from the passage?**

Help

In your answer you should comment on:

a what Dag says and does
b how different Dag's response to the snake is from Binh's
c how Dag treats his wife.

2   The trip to a restaurant where she and Dag are offered snake wine and snake curry is just one of the events Maria Coffey includes in her book describing their travels in Vietnam.

How does Maria Coffey make this episode entertaining for her reader?

 Help

In your answer you should comment on:

a   what happens at the restaurant

b   how different people behave

c   the way Chin and events at his restaurant are described

d   what the reader learns about Vietnamese life

e   any words or phrases which struck you.

 Key points

When you are reading travel writing you should especially notice:

- how unfamiliar situations are described and experienced
- traditions of the country, and how they are described
- similarities and differences between cultures and people.

1   Very few of Maria Coffey's readers will have been faced with eating fresh snake or drinking snake wine themselves. Much of the interest of the passage comes from seeing how she and her husband handle such a strange situation. Look out for the detailed descriptions which allow the reader to picture the experience vividly.

2   In this passage a Vietnamese tradition is described of naming children to fool evil spirits. Maria does not comment on it, however, and in this way she shows respect for the Vietnamese. Although Maria includes detailed information about the Vietnamese way of life, she leaves it to the readers to form their own opinions about it.

3   One of the ways in which we become aware of similarities and differences between cultures and people in this passage is when Maria describes how the characters react differently to the live snake. Binh and Maria are wary, while Chin and Dag are much more relaxed.

The use of such contrasts makes the passage entertaining to read. It also helps us to see that people from different cultures may have different traditions and customs but they also have much in common. A person's reaction to snakes can depend as much upon their personality as where they live.

B22 Uriah Heep

David Copperfield is staying with a lawyer called Mr Wickfield and his daughter Agnes. One evening he tries to make friends with Uriah Heep, who is one of Mr Wickfield's employees.

On the surface Uriah seems modest (or 'umble') and quite a friendly sort of person, but David quickly finds that there's something rather unpleasant and irritating about Uriah Heep. See if you can work out what it is …

I found Uriah reading a great fat book, with such **demonstrative** attention, that his lanky forefinger followed up every line as he read, and made clammy tracks along the page (or so I fully believed) like a snail.

'You are working late to-night, Uriah,' says I.

5   'Yes, Master Copperfield,' says Uriah.

As I was getting on the stool opposite, to talk to him more conveniently, I observed that he had not such a thing as a smile about him, and that he could only widen his mouth and make two hard creases down his cheeks, one on each side, to stand for one.

10   'I am not doing office work, Master Copperfield,' said Uriah.

'What work, then?' I asked.

> **demonstrative:** *Uriah's movements point out that he is reading*

I am improving my legal knowledge, Master Copperfield,' said Uriah. 'I am going through *Tidd's Practice*. Oh, what a writer Mr Tidd is, Master Copperfield!'

15 My stool was such a tower of observation, that as I watched him reading on again, after this rapturous exclamation, and following up the lines with his forefinger, I observed that his nostrils, which were thin and pointed, with sharp dints in them, had a singular and most uncomfortable way of expanding and contracting themselves; that they seemed to twinkle instead
20 of his eyes, which hardly ever twinkled at all.

'I suppose you are quite a great lawyer?' I said, after looking at him for some time.

'Me, Master Copperfield?' said Uriah. 'Oh no! I'm a very umble person.'

It was no fancy of mine about his hands, I observed; for he frequently
25 ground the palms against each other as if to squeeze them dry and warm, besides often wiping them, in a stealthy way, on his pocket handkerchief.

'I am well aware that I am the umblest person going,' said Uriah Heep modestly; 'let the other be where he may. My mother is likewise a very umble person. We live in a numble abode, Master Copperfield, but we have much to
30 be thankful for. My father's calling was umble. He was a **sexton**.'

'What is he now?' I asked.

'He is the partaker of glory at present, Master Copperfield,' said Uriah Heep. 'But we have much to be thankful for. How much have I to be thankful for in living with Mr. Wickfield!'

35 I asked Uriah if he had been with Mr. Wickfield long?

'I have been with him going on four years, Master Copperfield,' said Uriah; shutting up his book, after carefully marking the place where he had left off. 'Since a year after my father's death. How much have I to be thankful for, in that! How much have I to be thankful for, in Mr. Wickfield's kind intention to
40 give me my articles, which would otherwise not lay within the umble means of mother and self!'

'Then, when your articled time is over, you'll be a regular lawyer, I suppose?' said I.

'With the blessing of Providence, Master Copperfield,' returned Uriah.

45 'Perhaps you'll be a partner in Mr. Wickfield's business, one of these days,' I said, to make myself agreeable; 'and it will be Wickfield and Heep, or Heep late Wickfield.'

> **sexton:** *a church clerk who was often the grave digger as well*

'Oh, no, Master Copperfield,' returned Uriah, shaking his head, 'I am much too umble for that!'

50   He certainly did look uncommonly like the carved face on the beam outside my window, as he sat, in his humility, eyeing me sideways, with his mouth widened, and the creases in his cheeks.

'Mr. Wickfield is a most excellent man, Master Copperfield,' said Uriah. 'If you have known him long, you know it, I am sure, much better than I can
55   inform you.'

I replied that I was certain he was; but that I had not known him long myself, though he was a friend of my aunt's.

'Oh, indeed, Master Copperfield,' said Uriah. 'Your aunt is a sweet lady, Master Copperfield!'

60   He had a way of writhing when he wanted to express enthusiasm, which was very ugly; and which diverted my attention from the compliment he had paid my relation, to the snaky twistings of his throat and body.

'A sweet lady, Master Copperfield!' said Uriah. 'She has a great admiration for Miss Agnes, Master Copperfield, I believe?'

65   I said 'Yes,' boldly; not that I knew anything about it, Heaven forgive me!

'I hope you have, too, Master Copperfield,' said Uriah. 'But I am sure you must have.'

'Everybody must have,' I returned.

'Oh thank you, Master Copperfield,' said Uriah Heep, 'for that remark! It is
70   so true! Umble as I am, I know it is *so* true! Oh thank you, Master Copperfield!'

He writhed himself quite off his stool in the excitement of his feelings, and, being off, began to make arrangements for going home.

'Mother will be expecting me,' he said, referring to a pale, inexpressive-faced watch
75   in his pocket, 'and getting uneasy; for though we are very umble, Master Copperfield, we are very much attached to one another. If you would come and see us, any
80   afternoon, and take a cup of tea at our lowly dwelling, mother would be as proud of your company as I should be.'

I said I should be glad
85   to come.

David Copperfield *by Charles Dickens*

Questions

1 Look at lines 1–20. What are David's first impressions of Uriah?

 Help

In your answer you should comment on:
- **a** what Uriah is doing
- **b** what Uriah tells David
- **c** how he addresses David
- **d** the way David describes Uriah.

2 Look at the rest of the passage, from line 21 to the end. How does the author build up a picture of Uriah as a character who is both unpleasant and irritating?

 Help

In your answer you should comment on:
- **a** what Uriah tells David about himself and his parents
- **b** what he has to say about David's Aunt, Mr Wickfield and Agnes
- **c** the way Uriah moves
- **d** the way Uriah speaks
- **e** how David reacts to him.

 Remember

If you are reading a text and the sentences seem long and tangled, then:
- read the text slowly and carefully
- work out one sentence at a time
- check whether rearranging the order of words or phrases will help you to understand the sentence better.

1   It is not just the way a character is described that matters, you can learn a lot more about a character from:
    a   what other characters say about him
    b   how other characters react to him
    c   what he says about himself
    d   the way he speaks and moves.

    The writer uses all of these to give a more vivid picture of what Uriah is like.

2   In the passage David is the one who tells us what he notices about Uriah. He says that Uriah reminds him of a snail, a snake and a wooden statue. David also tells us that Uriah's eyes do not twinkle but his nostrils do. This suggests that his nostrils are always damp. None of these comments makes Uriah seem at all attractive. He may be trying to appear polite, friendly, hardworking and modest but the details noticed by David, the viewpoint character, suggest that Uriah is cold and unpleasant.

3   When we listen carefully to what Uriah tells us about himself and his family, we realise that David is right to be wary of him. Uriah keeps telling us how humble he is (try counting how many times he says he is 'umble' in the passage) – but then he boasts about his humility.

4   Uriah's manner makes David feel uncomfortable. Yes, he is polite – too polite. David feels ill at ease when Uriah thanks him for what he said about Agnes. After all, why should Uriah feel it is necessary to thank him for saying that everyone must admire Agnes?

5   Uriah's movements give him away too. Even when he is saying something nice about another character, such as David's aunt, he writhes like a snake. Snakes are traditionally symbols of evil (think about the one in the Garden of Eden in the Bible story of Adam and Eve). Comparing Uriah to one just adds to our picture of him as someone untrustworthy.

Working under pressure

At some stage you are likely to answer questions about a passage under test conditions. Now that you have practised reading and understanding different kinds of texts, you should do well. Make sure you work within the time limit set and present your answers in the best possible way.

Units C1 and C2 are about working under test conditions. Units C3 and C4 are practice units, each containing a pair of texts and questions. You should aim to complete the work on both texts in an hour and work under test conditions.

Be prepared

1   Before you start a test make sure that you have all the equipment you need:
    - pens
    - pencils and colour pencils to mark the paper
    - rubber, pencil sharpener and ruler.

2   Find out as much as you can about the type of test you are sitting. Study past papers to find out how long the paper lasts and what type of things you will be asked to do.

3   Make sure you know where and when the test will take place. Try to arrive in plenty of time.

4   Keep calm before you go in – obviously you are bound to feel a little nervous but try to relax. When you get into the room and are seated, lay out your equipment so that you will be able to reach it easily, and make sure you can see a clock. (Wear your own watch if possible.)

Read the instructions

As soon as you are given the test paper, read the front cover and check that you have the right paper. Then read through all the instructions and carry them out carefully.

Read through the paper

You may be given a set time in which to read through the paper and to make notes. Even if you are not, it is a good idea to spend the first ten to fifteen minutes reading through the paper and marking it since this will help you work much more efficiently when you start writing your answers. The method below should help you make good use of that time.

1   **Read the whole paper through once**, quickly, so that you know what it contains.

2   Then read the first section's questions **before** you re-read the first text.

3   If a question says the answer is to be found only in certain lines then use a colour to underline the question and then use the same colour to put a ring around the lines mentioned.

4   Read through the first text more slowly and at this stage make notes in the margin, underline phrases, and so on, as you note any details which will be useful as you plan and write your answers.

5   Write your answers for the first section.

6   Repeat steps **2–5** as you work on the second section.

Practice

Copy the two verses below on to the centre of a clean page (they are taken from a poem which appears in full on page 52). Then make notes in the way suggested, as if you were preparing to answer the question below.

Biking free

Black tyres spin –
pattern's tread –
spokes flicker –
legs of lead.

5   Steel rim squeals –
brake blocks clasp –
squeeze as hard –
as a bully's grasp.

Question

1   How do the first two verses of *Biking free* make you aware of what hard work cycling is?

Read the questions carefully

If you are going to answer a question well, you have to be sure that you are giving the examiners the answer that they asked for.

1   Look for key words

When you read a question, pick out the most important words. Make sure you notice everything it asks you to cover.

Practice

The following questions are examples of the sort of questions you may be asked after reading a passage. The first question has been marked to show you how to pick out the key words. Read it through carefully and then try to do the same with the second question.

Question 1

In lines <u>1 to 30</u> Alex describes how he and his friends discovered the fire. What do we learn about <u>Alex's thoughts and feelings</u> in these lines?

In your answer you should comment upon:
- <u>what Alex does;</u>
- the <u>way he describes</u> the <u>fire</u>
- <u>how Alex is affected</u> by <u>what his friends do or say.</u>

Question 2

Now look again at the section from line 31 to the end of the passage. The horror of the situation increases for the friends once they discover that the stairs below them have collapsed. How is the feeling of increasing horror built up?

In your answer you should comment upon:
- how the scene below is described
- how Lia behaves
- the way the boys react to the sound of sirens.

2   Take any advice that is offered

You will often be told some of the things your answer should include. Use any check-list you are given as a start by making sure you cover all the points mentioned in it. Then add in any points of your own. You may find that the order of points suggested in the check-list is also a good order in which to write your answer.

C2 Writing good answers

Don't just start writing!

Although it is tempting to rush into answering the question as soon as you have found the information to put in it, you will produce a more impressive answer if you think about:

- whether you have all the information you need
- how to organise your ideas
- how to express yourself.

Have you got all you need?

Examiners are usually looking for evidence that you have understood what you have read – not proof that you can copy out chunks of the text!

Although quoting small parts of the text may be useful (if you go on to explain exactly what it is you are showing through using the quotation), the examiner will usually want you to:

a use your own words as far as possible

b show that you have thought about and understood the text

c use the text to prove the points you are making.

 Remember

You will not earn marks for including information or ideas that the examiner is not asking for. You may even lose marks because you have not kept to the point.

Practice

Mark the answers to the following question, which is taken from page 78. Give the best answer an A, the second best a B and the worst answer a C. Bear in mind the advice you have just been given about what an examiner is looking for, and explain your reasons for awarding the marks as you have.

Question

1 Why does Kitty dislike Gerald so much?

Answer 1

Kitty does not like Gerald because he behaves like he owns the place. He is taking over her home by turning off all the lights every time he comes round, and he comes round too much. He is taking over her family. He tells Mum what to wear, and he has won Jude over too.

Answer 2

Kitty does not like Gerald because he is her mother's boyfriend and he is always coming round to her house and turning off all the lights. But I think Mum is right to like him. He is nice to her and the girls, and he will make a good stepfather because he is happy to help Jude with her homework.

Answer 3

Kitty dislikes Gerald because she feels he
  'acts as if it owns the place'
and is trying to push his way into her family. She can see that her mother really likes him, and dislikes the way Gerald keeps 'goggling' at her mother. Kitty is also aware that Jude likes him and uses listening to him read the financial section of the paper as a way of getting a cuddle. It is very unsettling for Kitty. She does not like Gerald telling her mother what to wear and so trying to change her. She even dislikes the way that he is so predictable. He always turns the lights off when he comes in and says
  "There! That should slow the little electric wheel down to a sprint!"

Organise your answer

Once you are sure that you have understood the question and have enough to say, it is worth pausing for a moment to plan how best to write your answer.

- Help yourself by making brief notes on the order in which you will make your points.

- If the question contained suggestions about what you should include in your answer, make sure that you include these in your plan.

- At the end of planning your answer, check that you have actually answered the question and that you are *not* going to write about things which you were *not* asked for.

- Begin your answer by showing that you have understood what the question was asking for.

- As you write, keep showing that what you have to say is relevant and that you really are answering the question that was asked.

Express yourself well

1   Always write in **full sentences**. In an exam your style should be formal. A formal sentence should not begin with words like:

but, and, so, because, or

because these words are used to join sentences together.

2   Think about your **handwriting** even if you are in a hurry. After all, you cannot score marks if the examiner cannot read what you have written!

3   Watch your **spelling**. Learn the correct spelling of words that you know you often get wrong.

4   Think about **punctuation** as you write. Do not make your sentences too long, and take care to use marks such as apostrophes, quotation marks and commas correctly.

5   Make sure what you have written **makes sense**. If, as you read through what you have written, you realise it does not make sense then change it. After all, if you cannot understand what you have written then it is unlikely that the examiner will.

6   When you have finished, **check your work through carefully.**

Writing about the text

1   When you are explaining how a word or detail works in a passage you can write:

(*The word or detail*)   **shows** that   (*and then explain what it shows*).

For example: *Calling it 'hell' shows that it was an evil place.*

2   Some different words to use in the place of 'shows' are:

- hints
- implies
- indicates
- infers
- means
- demonstrates
- signals
- warns
- insinuates
- suggests

For example: *'Chilling sight' suggests that it made people's blood run cold.*

Make sure you know exactly what a word means before you use it.

3   When you are writing about a detail or word, explain **how** it creates the effect you have noticed.

Think about what the word means and then look for possible reasons, such as:

- what the word suggests, hints at, or reminds you of
- how that word fits in to the rest of the phrase you are quoting
- the sound of the word or phrase
- what emotions or feelings the word creates.

4   In the example below, the phrase in **bold** type is examined in detail. This will give you some idea of the sorts of things you can say about a text.

Example

… the scarves which were **waved in victory, shaken in challenge, or swung like maces in aggression, were just hanging there for the moment, threatening.**

Explanation

The way the scarves were held shows how the people carrying the scarves were feeling.

The scarves were '**waved in victory**'. The use of the word 'waved' implies a mood of excitement in keeping with the idea of celebrating a victory.

Next we are told that the scarves were '**shaken in challenge**'. This indicates a big change in mood because 'shaken' is a much stronger verb than 'waved'. Since you shake a fist at someone when you are angry, it fits in with the idea that the people carrying the scarves were looking for a fight. This is also reflected in the word 'challenge'.

The worst action described is '**swung like maces in aggression**'. Using the word 'swung' warns of a lack of control. It also speaks of energy – you would want to get out of the way of scarves wielded like that. The scarves are compared to medieval weapons called 'maces', which were sticks with a hard metal end used in battle. This signals that the scarves may be knotted at one end so that they will hurt the people they hit. There is no doubt about the feeling behind the way the scarves were used now – 'aggression' is a strong motive which usually leads to violence.

The description of the scarves reveals the mood of the people carrying them. It leads us to agree with the final statement that while the scarves were '**just hanging**' they seem '**threatening**'. The word 'hanging' seems much closer to the idea of fighting than of victory. It also contains the idea of waiting, which adds to the sense that something bad is going to happen soon.

C3 Down and out

Instructions

You should spend ten minutes reading through this unit. You may make notes but you should not start writing your answers until after this period of time.

You should answer <u>all</u> of the questions on both passages.

Check your work carefully.

Section A

The following extract is set in America. Mother Peters and Uncle Daniels have fostered many children, including Edith Jackson and 14–year old Kenneth. Unexpectedly a tramp (or wino) has come to the door and asked for a glass of water. Mother Peters has left him outside and gone to fetch one. Edith describes what happens next …

Mother Peters pushed by me when she came back with the water. She opened the door, but the wino had been waiting. The glass in her hand put her off balance. The wino pushed hard with his shoulder and in no time managed to worm himself inside. He stood with his back against the wall.

5 'You carn't put me out,' he said to her face. 'No, yer carn't put me out. I got rights. I got rights.' His voice went shrill. He trembled, and sweat ran down his beaten face. 'I got a right to be here. You hear? A right, ma'am.'

He kept on talking like he intended everyone to hear. And they did. The kids came out on the landing upstairs. Uncle Daniels walked out of the living
10 room, and when he took in what was going on he rushed to help Mother Peters. But she shook her head. She held out the glass of water to Uncle Daniels, but he didn't take it. I could see Uncle Daniels didn't understand what was happening no more than I did.

The wino, one shoulder jammed against the door frame, refused to be
15 moved. 'Yer carn't put me out. Let me be. Let me be.'

Then he looked up the stairs and called, 'Son – son. Help me. Don't let them send me away.'

There had to be some sense in that scene. And all at once it came through to me – to us. We all looked at Kenneth. Kenneth, his face pale, his blue eyes
20 staring, walked down the steps, taking them one at a time, like a child learning to walk. Slow. One at a time.

Like bodies made of wax, we stood still as he came down. And in the way of things that seem never to end, he reached bottom.

'Son.' The man swallowed. 'I – I brought a li'l somethin' for yer.' The wino
25 fumbled in his baggy pants pockets and brought out a tiny racing car – the plastic kind bought in candy stores.

The tall, broad, blond, blue-eyed giant of a fourteen-year-old took a few steps towards his father, holding out his hand. It closed around the little car. He held it to his chest. *Funny*. No one laughed.

30 'Jist a li'l somethin', me lad.' The wino tried to smile. 'You know? A li'l somethin' – want you to understand – I ain't forgot. Lad – I ain't forgot.'

Quiet strained us, drained us. I felt my blood beating in my head. I knew it sort of beat in time with the clock in the living room. The quiet hurt as the boy held on to his little car. Squeezed it so the axle fell off. Then the wheels.
35 The plastic melted into a ball. He kept squeezing.

The father got tired. He looked around, smiling, wanting to bring us into the scene. He had won, his sick smile said. He had come to see his son and he had seen him. No one, but no one, had stopped him. No one had been able to. We were the witnesses.

40 'That's what I come to tell yer. I ain't forgot yer.' The needle had stuck. The dialogue ended. He backed to the door.

'Pop. Pop – '

At the sound the man shrank. Drew into himself. Small. Smaller. Tried to melt out the door. But the door was closed. It didn't open to his fumbling hand.

45 'Pop – take me with you.'

The fumbling hands grew frantic, trying to turn the knob.

'I – I –' The wino swallowed, kept swallowing, the skin riding his throat. 'Well, yer know, son – the law –'

'I don't care about the law!' Kenneth's voice rose. He was getting
50 hysterical. 'I want you! I got to be with you!'

' I – I – Yer know I been looking for us a place ...' His mouth quivered. 'I – been looking for us a place ...'

'I don't care about a place.' Kenneth's face grew red; his eyes looked feverish. 'I want to be where you are. Wherever you are!'

55 The little man looked around for help. His eyes shifted fast from one face to the next. His worn smile was shaky now, showing he was doubtful he had won. His searching hands found the knob. He turned it, opened the door. Escape. He had to escape. Trapped. His eyes begged Kenneth to let him go. Let him out. 'I – I – I'll send for yer. Soon's I get us a place. Swear ...'

60   Licked his lips. Thirsty. But not for the water Mother Peters still held.
Real thirsty. He needed a drink for his life. 'Ma'am,' he said. Respectful. 'Yer
got maybe – a buck – fifty cents? I – carfare, ma'am …'

Uncle Daniels dug in his pocket for a dollar. 'Thank yer. Thank yer kindly.'
He jerked the door open. Made the front porch.

65   Kenneth rushed after him. Stopped him. 'Pop! Pop!'

He caught the little man on the top step, held him. Kenneth fell to his
knees, holding his father, his head buried in the tired, wasted stomach. 'Don't
leave me. Don't leave me. Take me with you.' Kenneth's big body shook,
crying. 'I'll look after you, Pop. I'll look after you.'

70   'Ple–ee–ease!'

The weird cry released us. We rushed to the door. Peered out. Man and boy
had disappeared. We heard running feet, and I ran. Ran in the direction of
the footsteps. I knew the way of wine and winos. And I knew the way of boys,
the way they got lost forever while running.

Edith Jackson by Rosa Guy

Section A questions

*Answer question **1** and question **2**.*

Refer to words and phrases in the passage to support your ideas.

1   Look again at lines 1–13.

   What do you learn in these lines about the thoughts and feelings of the family members about the arrival of the wino?

   In your answer you should comment on:
   - how Mother Peters responds to the tramp
   - how Edith describes the tramp
   - what the rest of the family do when they hear the tramp.

2   Now look again at the section from line 14 to the end of the passage.

   How does the writer build up the sense that Kenneth has been desperately hoping that his father would come and collect him one day?

   In your answer you should comment on:
   - how Kenneth reacts to seeing his father
   - how Kenneth handles the toy
   - what Kenneth and his father say to each other
   - how Kenneth reacts as his father is leaving.

Section B

Study the newspaper article below.

TB and the cut-price, swept away, disposable Britain

Dreaded disease is back on our streets

Nineties Britain: As a sweeper appears, homeless people sleeping in doorways on London's Strand must wake to face another day

Out of the 68,000 homeless people in Britain, one in 50 now has tuberculosis, according to the charity Crisis

by NICKI POPE, Medical Correspondent

It was the killer lung disease we believed had gone for good. Tuberculosis – TB for short.

Over 50 years ago, TB struck down rich and poor alike. Then, it seemed, the march of medicine wiped out the disease in this country.

Now it is back. But this time the victims are the poorest of our poor, those without home or hope.

As they camp on the streets of John Major's Britain, in their cardboard boxes, their plastic sheets and tattered blankets, the 68,000 homeless people are 200 times more likely than the rest of us to get TB. One in every 50 of those sleeping rough, or in hostels for the homeless, now has it.

A survey by the charity Crisis shows TB at its highest rate for 30 years among those at the bottom of the social scale.

And Crisis says it is a growing menace which the government can no longer hope to sweep aside.

Worrying

In London last summer, X-ray tests found 12 new cases among 600-plus hostel and day-centre users.

Crisis director Mark Scothern said: 'This problem is unacceptable as we approach the 21st century.'

British Lung Foundation director Ian Govendir says:

'Tuberculosis is not a disease of the history books. It's worrying that it is growing among the homeless.'

A cost-cutting government cannot console itself that this evil affects only a limited 'underclass'. TB is highly infectious. It can be cured by antibiotics. Without them it can kill.

Dr Ken Citron, of London's National Heart and Lung Hospital, warned that if TB got out of hand, it could spread to the rest of the population.

'Generally, TB needs close and prolonged contact,' he said. 'But those working with homeless people should be protected by vaccination.

'*Anybody can get it.*'

Flashback to 1944: Glasgow women line up to be X-rayed as part of a mass campaign to beat the lung disease

Today

Section B questions

Read the article carefully. The article tries to show readers that tuberculosis (known as TB) is becoming a serious problem in Britain today.

Now answer question 3.

Refer to words and phrases in the article to support your ideas.

3   **In what ways does the article try to persuade readers to care that TB is becoming a serious problem in Britain?**

In your answer you should comment on:
- choice of pictures and layout
- what the article says about the disease
- how TB affected people in the past
- what experts are saying about TB in Britain now.

C4 Time to act

Instructions

You should spend ten minutes reading through this unit. You may make notes but you should not start writing your answers until after this period of time.

You should answer all of the questions on both passages.

Check your work carefully.

Section A

A nuclear power station is going to be built near to where Josie and her family live. Up until now Josie has been campaigning legally against it. Now she and her friends are about to do something illegal. They are going to lie across the road to act as a human barrier to stop lorries getting onto the building site. Naturally, once they do this, the police have to arrest them for breaking the law.

Josie and her friends did not, though, have permission to lie in the road. Twenty of them had decided to do it.

The demonstration had broken up, the crowd was dispersing, making its way, in a more straggly fashion than it had come, back towards the town.
5 The attention of the police was diverted.

'There's going to be an accident here, I can see that,' said the sergeant and went striding off as a lorry lurched around the corner sending people scuttling into the side.

'Right?' said Jack.

10 'Take care!' said Emma.

'Bring us a nail file,' said Josie.

The twenty went quickly across the road. Joining hands, they stretched out across the site entrance and lay down.

Immediately, the alarm was raised. A shout went up from a constable and
15 the sergeant came lumbering back, his face purpling, with several other constables at his heels. And behind them came the lorry, its back heaped high with concrete blocks.

The sergeant raised his loud-hailer to his mouth. 'I would advise you to clear the roadway.' His voice boomed out over their heads. 'This is private
20 ground belonging to the Electricity Board and you are contravening a bye-law by trespassing. You are also causing obstruction and, for that, I must warn you, you could be charged.'

They did not answer. They continued to lie on the ground. Marge lay close to Josie, their arms touching, their hands still clasped. Swivelling her eyes
25 round, Josie saw that her friend was staring upward, at the cab of the lorry, which had come to a halt. Out of the window poked the head of Marge's father. He was staring down at his daughter as if he could not quite believe what he saw.

The sky at the back of the lorry was dark now, Josie noticed, very dark.
30 She shivered, feeling suddenly chilled. Time seemed almost to have stood still. And it had gone strangely quiet. She thought of the people, often groups of women, who during the Highland Clearances in Scotland in the 18th and 19th centuries had stood in the roadway obstructing the path of the sheriffs' officers who carried writs of eviction.

35 And then the rain came, mild in the beginning but swelling soon to a torrent. They brought up their arms to shield their faces.

'Right, men!' Josie heard the sergeant cry above the sound of the rain. By now she thought she would recognise his voice in a crowded football stadium.

And so the constables came forward to remove them. The demonstrators
40 did not resist – they had all been agreed about that – but neither did they help. They let themselves go limp, like dead weights. Some of the police were relatively gentle, others were not. Josie did not get a gentle one, had not expected to. Somehow or other, she felt that she would be picked out. It was the sergeant himself who came for her.

45 As he pulled her by the shoulders along the ground he caught hold of her hair, perhaps by mistake, perhaps not, but he did not let go. She bit her lip hard. She would not scream, she *would not*. He saw her pain and she saw the look on his face. Serves you right, it said: you asked for it.

Within minutes, the twenty had been dragged across the road and laid out
50 on the ground opposite. The police towered over them, defying them now to get to their feet. The sergeant released Josie's hair and the pain stopped. She closed her eyes for a moment with the relief, not caring how wet she was.

Opening her eyes, she saw a circle of faces around them. Not all of them were crowned with police helmets. A number of people had come running
55 back when they'd heard there was trouble.

'Are you all right?' Mr Greig called out.

'Keep back please, everyone!' shouted the sergeant. 'Right back!'

Josie came up into a sitting position and hugged her knees to her chin. The rain was easing. Thank goodness for that at least. Her backbone felt as if
60 a scraper had been taken to it. She should have had her anorak hood up and her hair tucked into it. She would know better next time.

'How are you doing?' she asked Marge.

'Getting dragged along the road was nothing compared to the look my dad gave me! I might be out in the street with you looking for digs.'

65 'Almost two thousand,' said Khalil, producing his calculator. He had decided to join them in the end, after a great deal of heart searching.

They stopped talking when they saw two police wagons approaching.

'Are you going to walk or do you want to be carried?' asked the sergeant.

No co-operation, that was what they had decided. The constables returned.
70 The girls they picked up and carried into the wagon, the boys were dragged.

'It's like the Tokyo underground in here,' said Josie. They could hardly move their arms in the crush inside the wagon.

Two constables got in at the back beside them, another two sat up front with the driver. Steam rose from their wet clothes and clouded the windows.
75 They set off back towards town.

The Guilty Party by *Joan Lingard*

Section A questions

*Answer question **1** and question **2**.*

Refer to words and phrases in the passage to support your ideas.

1 Look again at lines 1–52.

   What impression do you gain of the protesters as the demonstration goes on?

   In your answer you should comment on:
   - how the protesters behave
   - the change in the weather
   - Josie's thoughts and feelings
   - the way the police respond, and how they treat the protesters.

2 Now look again at the section from line 53 to the end of the passage.

   The protesters have been dragged away from the main road and are about to be taken down to the police station.

   Explain the mixed thoughts and feelings of the protesters.

   In your answer you should comment on:
   - what Josie thinks and feels
   - what Marge is worrying about
   - what Khalil says
   - how they respond to the police now.

Section B

Study the 'Friends of the Earth' leaflet which has been set out on pages 153–157, then turn to the question on page 158.

1

2

Look forward to a better future

For thousands upon thousands of years, the Earth has sustained a wonderfully rich and interconnected web of **life.**

Now one single species - humankind - is putting it all at risk.

5 The world's forests are **disappearing**... our air and water are no longer clean and pure... species are **dying out** at a terrifying rate... toxic **waste** is piling up... people everywhere **suffer** from pollution and environmental damage.

10 It needn't be like this. For twenty years Friends of the Earth has led the way in putting forward **positive solutions** to these and many other environmental problems.

15 Thanks to the support of tens of thousands of people who share our conviction that the natural world and all living things should be treated with wisdom and respect, we've won some tremendous **victories.**

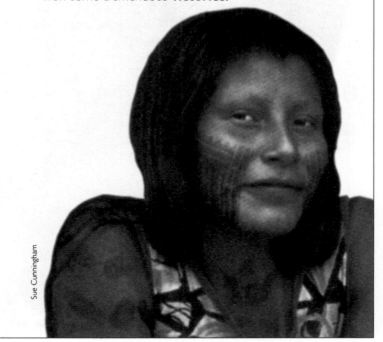

Sue Cunningham

3

Our successes are your successes

With the support of people like you, and backed by careful research, Friends of the Earth has: **persuaded** Parliament to pass three major environmental Acts that we first drafted... **forced** UK aerosol makers to stop using ozone-destroying CFCs... **pressured** the Government to speed up the removal of pesticides and nitrates from drinking water using the European and High Courts... **pioneered** practical renewable energy and waste-recycling schemes... **stopped** the hunting of otters in Britain... **persuaded** the EC to ban the sale of all whale products... **convinced** the Government to cancel 32 new nuclear power stations... **saved** wildlife reserves from development... **forced** major corporations to abandon destructive projects in tropical rainforests... **exposed** health-threatening traffic pollution levels... **uncovered** the location of thousands of secret toxic waste dumps... **persuaded** the largest DIY stores to stop selling peat from nature reserves and mahogany from tropical rainforests.

Become a Friends of the Earth supporter and become part of this **powerful force** for environmental protection.

20

25

30

35

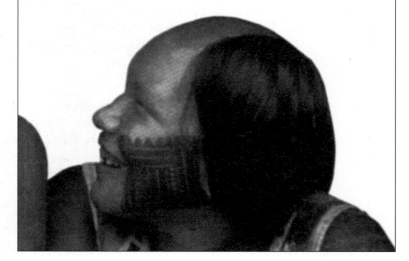

4

40

Become a Friend of the Earth

Our supporters are to thank for every success we score on behalf of the natural world.

They finance almost all of our work. When you consider what we are up against - governments, powerful industrial interests and the huge resources at their disposal - you can appreciate how important this funding is and how much it achieves.

45

We use all our supporters' contributions wisely. Less than 8% of our income is spent on administration.

50

As the pace of environmental destruction accelerates, it's all too easy to get downhearted. Even to give up on it all! But we _are_ making progress, and a better future _is_ possible.

55

And that's where Friends of the Earth comes in. Its track record in developing positive solutions to all those problems — internationally, nationally and locally — is second to none. It's a real force for change in a world that's stuck in a dangerous rut.

60

65

It's your support that makes this work possible — and its needed now more than ever before.

Jonathon Porritt

70

Jonathon Porritt
Special Adviser to Friends of the Earth

5

Five good reasons to support Friends of the Earth

We are effective: our campaigns get politicians and industry to take action - through persuasive argument, lobbying and use of the law when necessary.   75

We are authoritative: our pioneering research is widely used by governments, commerce, the media and other environmental organizations.

We inform: we publish a broad range of information to   80
help everyone find out about and take action on environmental problems that affect them.

We are independent: we work with all political parties, but are aligned to none.

We innovate at all levels: from our participation in   85
Friends of the Earth International to the work carried out by over 250 local groups, we are uniquely placed to mobilize public opinion and campaign successfully - locally, nationally and internationally.

"Technical dialogue is often better from   90
Friends of the Earth than from industry."

Dr David Slater, Chief Inspector,
Her Majesty's Inspectorate of Pollution.

Joseph Drivas The Image Bank

"About 15 years ago,
someone told me that   95
Friends of the Earth's
campaigners were
likely to know more
about their subjects than
the relevant Minister.   100
I didn't believe it.
Since then I have found
that this has usually been
the case. Friends of the
Earth has maintained its   105
reputation as a reliable
and indispensable source
of information."

Geoffrey Lean,
Environment Correspondent,   110
The Independent on Sunday.

Section B questions

Read the leaflet carefully. The leaflet tries to persuade people to become a supporter of Friends of the Earth, an organisation which wants to make sure that the environment is protected.

Now answer question 3.

Refer to words and phrases in the article to support your ideas.

3 **In what ways does the leaflet try to persuade people to become supporters of Friends of the Earth?**

In your answer you should comment on:
- the choice of pictures and layout
- the impression you are given of Friends of the Earth
- what Friends of the Earth say about their supporters
- the way language is used
- whether you think the leaflet would persuade someone to donate money to, and become a supporter of, Friends of the Earth.

Glossary

alliteration	the repetition of consonants (letters other than a, e, i, o, u) in two or more words near each other. For example, *the **t**atty **t**rainers*.
assonance	the repetition of vowel sounds, or the rhyming of them. For example, *l**e**gs of l**ea**d*. (See page 52 for other examples of assonance).
atmosphere	the mood or feeling the writer has given a place or situation. It could be tense, peaceful, excited, creepy and so on (see page 96).
conflict	a struggle between characters or ideas (see page 79).
contrast	a striking difference between two things (see page 109).
dialogue	conversation spoken by characters.
description	tells the reader what people, places or things are like (see Unit A4, starting on page 24).
fact	a statement which can be proved (see page 28).
image	a picture created by words which helps the reader to imagine what the writer is describing more fully. The two main types of imagery are **metaphor** and **simile**.
metaphor	a type of **image**. The writer speaks of something *as if it actually were* something else, for example, *The moon is a balloon*. The words 'like' and 'as' are *not* used, which is different from a **simile**.
narrative	the telling of a story (see page 85).
mood	this is created through the **tone** or **atmosphere** of a piece of writing. It could be happy, sad, positive, romantic and so on.
onomatopoeia	a word whose sound echoes its meaning. For example, *crash*, *snap*, *rustle*.
opinion	what someone believes (see page 28).
pace	the speed at which sentences can be read (see page 112).
personification	the writer speaks of a non-living object as if it were a person. For example, *the door **groaned** on its hinges*.

plot the series of events which take place in a story.

quotation the name given to words copied exactly from a text. The action of copying part of a text and including it in your own writing is called quoting (see page 43).

repetition when the same word or phrase is repeated. Repetition is used by writers to make the reader take particular notice.

rhymes words which end in similar sounds. For example, *tray, bay, say*.

rhythm a pattern of emphasised sounds (or beats) in a line.

scene setting describing the place or situation in which the events of a story happen (see page 55).

stage directions tell the reader how to read or act out the lines in a drama script. Also give other information the reader needs to understand about how the scene should be presented, for example, describing setting, props and so on (see page 73).

setting where events takes place – the place, the time and so on.

simile a type of **image**. In a simile the writer compares something with another thing using the words 'as' or 'like'. For example, *It looked absurdly like a very large jelly baby*.

stanza a verse in a poem.

symbol a form of **imagery** in which something is used to represent something else. For example a snake may be used as a symbol of evil (see page 134).

tension a sense of expectancy or excitement as the reader waits for something to happen (see pages 85 and 96).

tone an overall mood or feeling of a piece of writing. For example, serious, mocking, persuasive and so on (see page 18).

viewpoint the point of view from which the story is told (see page 85).